The Life
of
Emily Peake

For Jann Klim,
whose roots
lie very near
to Emily's

Enjoy!

Jann P 959

March, 2004

The Life of Emily Peake

One Dedicated Ojibwe

by

Jane Pejsa

NODIN PRESS

Illustrations

Unless otherwise noted, pictures are courtesy
Emily Peake's niece Jacqueline Heine. MHS indicates the
collections of the Minnesota Historical Society.

ISBN- 1 - 932472-01-0

Nodin Press, a division of Micawber's, Inc.
530 N. Third Street, Suite 120
Minneapolis, Minnesota 55401

For my husband Arthur,
whose support and friendly criticism
continue to energize me

Contents

Acknowledgments

Seven years after the death of Emily Peake, the timing seems right to record her life story. Surely it is not too early, for many of the undone pieces out of Emily's life and work have in the meantime been resolved. Nor is it too late. Most of those closest to Emily— her family, childhood friends, colleagues, acquaintances, even her political adversaries—are still alive and pleased to share memories of this extraordinary human being.

Among the thirty-some people with whom I have spoken— most of them in extensive interviews—all but a handful knew Emily personally. They and others have also provided extensive insight into Emily's White Earth roots and the Twin Cities Indian community into which she was born. In addition, they have provided rare documents relating to this history. Important documents are cited in the Bibliography.

First and foremost, I wish to acknowledge with deepest gratitude the support of Jacqueline Heine, Emily's niece and keeper of her surviving papers. Without Jacqueline's generous cooperation this tale could not have been written.

Each of the following has contributed in one way or another to the collective memory regarding Emily Peake's roots, her life, and her legacy: Deborah Adair, Frances Anderson, Amy Aspinwall Flocken, Alberta Bedeau Norris, Clyde Bellecourt, Juanita Blackhawk, Pauline Brunette Danforth, Gertrude Buckanaga, Priscilla Buffalohead, Lorraine Campbell, Bob Danforth, Frances Fairbanks, Norby Fairbanks Blake, Andy Favorite, Lou Gelfand, Myles Goddard, Judge Isabel Gomez, Grant Heine, Thomas Hodne, Margaret Kränz, Jeanne Krueger, Joe La Garde, James Longie (Chief Blackbird), Larry Martin, Deborah Miller, Evon

Mims Shahan, Hy Rosen, Inez Sandness, Mariana Shulstad, Claricy Smith, Nancy Smith Falkum, Dee Tvedt, Vernell Wabasha, Lloyd Wittstock, and Joyce Yellowhammer. I hereby gratefully acknowledge these contributions and extend my thanks to each one named above. If by error I have omitted someone, please accept my thanks nevertheless.

Special thanks to Barbara Field, who has edited the manuscript and smoothed out any inconsistencies that might have crept in; also to John Toren who has designed and deftly composed the book.

The tale would have been very incomplete had I not had access to a variety of repositories where so much important history lies. Thus I acknowledge with gratitude the following institutions, each of which yielded gems that have been incorporated into this biography: Cumberland County Historical Society, Carlisle Pennsylvania; Madison County Historical Society, Canton Mississippi; Minneapolis Public Library History Collection, Minneapolis; Minnesota Historical Society Library, St. Paul; National Archives and Records Administration, Washington, D.C.; Office of Senator Paul Wellstone, Minneapolis; Smithsonian National Anthropological Archives, Washington, D.C.; *Star Tribune* Archives, Minneapolis; U.S. Department of Justice (FBI), Washington, D.C.; U.S. Army Intelligence and Security Command, Fort Meade, Maryland; University of Minnesota Libraries, Minneapolis; and University of Wisconsin Library: Special Collections, Stevens Point, Wisconsin.

This project has been supported in part by a grant from the Minnesota Historical Society with funds provided by the State of Minnesota. I hereby express my great appreciation for this support.

JANE PEJSA, MINNEAPOLIS

The Emily Peake Memorial Garden

One might well say it is an unlikely spot, but there it lies on a vacant lot between an asphalt parking lot and a red brick apartment building in a neighborhood of older apartment buildings—this garden of annuals and perennials created by the Stevens Square community. The garden is truly a neighborhood enterprise. There aren't many gardens in the area, for the brick and stone buildings take up much of the land, and what's left over is mostly parking tarmac. Yet residents and building owners have succeeded in turning the vacant lot into a garden with hosta, columbine, phlox, the inevitable yellow and orange day lilies, and more. They have made paths, cultivated the earth, planted, weeded, and created this unlikely oasis in memory of Emily Peake, the Ojibwe mixed-blood.

The garden began informally the year Emily died. The plantings prospered. The vacant lot thus became an inspiration for other gardens and even a source of transplants, all because that was the way of Emily Peake. Then, six years after her death, following a lush garden summer, the community of Stevens Square decided to make it official—a formal dedication of the Emily Peake Memorial Garden.

So it was that someone asked me, "Who was Emily Peake?" And although I live not that far from Stevens Square and pride myself on being familiar with more than a bit of Minneapolis history, I was forced to say, "I don't know." Now, almost two years later, I do know who Emily was. I invite you, dear Reader, to meet this extraordinary woman and discover her rich and complex world. The likes of Emily Louise Peake, the Ojibwe mixed-blood, will not soon come by again.

JANE PEJSA, MINNEAPOLIS

xi

Emily Peake's Family Tree

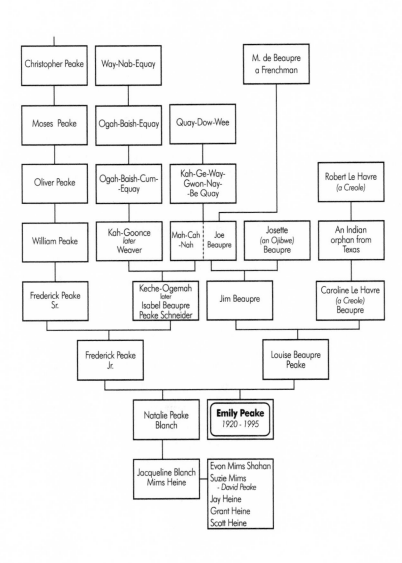

The Life
of
Emily Peake

Prologue

When the Earth was new, the Anishinaubag lived,*
congregated on the shores of a great salt water.
—Day-Doge[1]

July 4th, 1993. It was a rainy, drizzly, misty, Monday—hardly a typical "Fourth," but that made no difference. The weekend had been extraordinary. On Friday Emily Peake and her niece Jackie, along with two of Jackie's children, had driven up to the White Earth Ojibwe Reservation to attend the Peake family reunion. The Peakes were originally Yankees from the East. In the mid-nineteenth century five Peake brothers had come out to Minnesota "Indian country." All but one stayed, mostly taking Ojibwe wives. In the course of time many of their mixed-blood descendants had scattered about in the world, yet a large number still called White Earth "home." In fact this year more than 50, including Emily's little family, had attended the reunion. They called it the best ever.

Emily left White Earth early that Monday morning, for she intended to make an important stop along the way to Minneapolis—Crow Wing State Park, six miles south of Brainerd, where the Crow Wing and Mississippi rivers meet. On reaching the park, the little band of travelers left its auto in the parking area off the highway. Then, in the still misty morning, they climbed a forested

---

*Anishinabe, Anishinahbay, Anishinaubag, Anishinabay, Anishinaabe, and Anishinaabeg (plural) are all transliterations of the word the Ojibwe use when referring to their own people.

3

hill that they had climbed many times before. At the top was a bench from which one can view the valley and the rivers below. As on every other visit to Crow Wing, Emily first complained about the principal interpretive plaque, which chronicles the great Ojibwe-Dakota battle that took place at this site. Why always dredge up this past? In Emily's world the Ojibwe and Dakota of the Twin Cities were a team, battling together to achieve a better life for their People.

Yet Crow Wing was also a place of remembrance. During its brief heyday Crow Wing had been the greatest trading center in Central Minnesota, a place where the Yankee entrepreneurs set up shop and the Indian families set up a village. In fact Emily's great uncle Ebeneezer Peake, an Episcopal Missionary, had built a church on this very hilltop; and her Ojibwe grandmother Keche-Ogemah spent several years of her childhood here at Crow Wing. Later she and Emily's grandfather, Fred Peake, would be married at this site. And Emily's father—Fred Jr.—would be born and baptized here, before the family moved to White Earth. That was in 1871, the same year the railroad came through. Unfortunately, those in charge had located an easier crossing of the Mississippi six miles upstream from Crow Wing, where they founded the new town of Brainerd. Within two years Crow Wing was a ghost town, its church abandoned. By the time Emily herself first visited the site nothing remained of the town but a few gravestones.

From her hilltop bench Emily cautioned her companions never to forget their forebears. So long as they called forth the name of Grandfather Fred Peake, along with his mother Keche-ogemah, and her mother Kahgoonce, they would know whence they all came. Like these two women, and like Papa, and like Emily herself, her niece Jackie's family too belonged to the Crane clan. They should not forget that even to this day, like the crane with its far-reaching call, those of the Crane clan have strong voices. They are said to be the orators of the tribe.

All this Emily recounted from her bench on the overlook. The listeners had probably heard it before, more than a few times. Still it was their tradition and their *dodem*.* That's what made it special. Some day, promised Emily, she would write it all down, but not quite yet. There was still too much work to be done.

Now, having returned down the hill to the picnic shelter close to the highway, Emily and Jackie set up a little lunch, mostly with leftovers from the Peake Reunion—those wonderful traditional foods: wild rice cooked in beef broth, also dried venison and the ubiquitous fried bread, each one calling up memories from the past.

Just then a second auto pulled into the parking area. Emily recognized the young woman immediately—Pauline Brunette, now Danforth—also an Ojibwe with White Earth roots. Pauline and husband Bob were on their way back to Minneapolis from Duluth. They had stopped just to read the historic plaque, but finding Emily there, they stayed on to reminisce about how it had all begun and what it might all become in the future. Emily made reference to her favorite Anishinabe legend. Pauline could smile a bit, for she too had grown up with the tale.

> When Gitchee Munedoo made up his mind to create a man, he took in his hands some earth and rubbed it together in his palms, and behold a man was formed. The Spirit below the earth, who is a very great spirit with heavy locks of white hair, said to Gitchee Munedoo in council, "What are you going to do with only one man?"
>
> In answer to this Gitchee Munedoo took another handful of earth and rubbed his hands together, and behold, a woman was formed, and he said, "This person shall be the fruit of the earth and the seed from which the Indian race shall come and that is how the Indian race began." [2]

And so we begin where Emily left off, for she never did find the time to write it all down. Until her death less than two years later, Emily Peake's energies were directed to the future of her People.

---

* Dodem, a variation of totem—an object in nature that, for some native peoples, defines kinship.

Out of the Mists

Mixed-bloods and *full-bloods:* How curious are these words that surfaced in the mid-19th century. Yet how important they once were. When it came to treaties and land settlements, the categories had immense ramifications. Thus the roots of Emily Peake are best addressed in the language of the times. Emily was a mixed-blood. Both her parents were mixed-bloods. Emily's paternal grandmother Keche-ogemah was a mixed-blood, while her paternal grandfather, Frederick Peake, Sr., was the non-Indian in the family. And even then there were rumors that somewhere in his distinguished lineage lurked a Native American mother out of some obscure tribe. Emily's maternal grandfather James Beaupre was a mixed-blood. Her maternal grandmother Caroline Le Havre was also a mixed-blood, though out of a tribe far removed from the Anishinabe.

Keche-ogemah
Emily Peake's grandmother (1847-1929)

Emily's grandmother was born in 1847 at the Sandy Lake Ojibwe settlement on the Mississippi River. Her full name was Keche-ogemah-wuhb-equay. She was the daughter of Kah-goonce, who was the daughter of Ogah-baish-cum-equay, who was the daughter of Ogah-baish-equay, who was the daughter of Way-nab-equay. How do we know all of this? Because before Kah-goonce gave up her daughter in 1862, she taught her the names, lest the child forget whence her mother came.

And whence came Kah-goonce? We know that her ancestors were in the first wave of the Ojibwe migration from Lake Superior to the Mississippi River valley. We know that in the 1730s her band established the first Ojibwe power base west of the Mississippi, at Sandy Lake, and that its headmen—two generations of Chief Hole-in-the-Day—were signers of all the important treaties involving Ojibwe lands. These included the 1847 treaty signed at Fond du Lac, by which the Mississippi bands gave up most of central

St. Columba Mission at Gull Lake
MHS sketch from 1856, photo by Ralph D. Cleveland

Minnesota with the expectation that the land would be reserved for the Menominee and Winnebago tribes, an expectation that was betrayed by the United States government.

Keche-ogemah was born that same year to the seventeen-year-old maiden Kah-goonce. According to early records, the infant's father was one Mah-cah-nah Beaupre, whose mother was Kah-ge-way-gwon-nay-be-quay, daughter of Quay-dow-wee and cousin of the famed medicine man Day-Doge. Mah-cah-nah's father was the "Frenchman Beaupre." In those years, the appellation probably referred to a family of French traders who, a hundred years earlier, had settled in with the Ojibwe on the south shore of Lake Superior.

Most likely Mah-cah-nah's mixed-blood father and Mah-cah-nah himself were also in the business of trade, for the shores of Sandy Lake were the start of the legendary Savanna Portage, which connected the Mississippi headwaters to Lake Superior.

Quite possibly Kah-goonce attended some sort of school as a child. The first school ever established in Minnesota was a mission school founded in 1831 at the Sandy Lake village. By the time Keche-ogemah was of school age, however, this school was long gone. Yet if Kah-goonce once attended school, then it is not difficult to extrapolate that Keche-ogemah also may have learned English, as well as the rudiments of reading and writing. This would have set both mother and daughter apart from many others in their band.

At age fourteen, Keche-ogemah was obliged to give up her Ojibwe name; she was thereafter to be known as Isabel Elizabeth Beaupre. To understand how this all came about, one must begin with Ebeneezer Peake, an Episcopal priest from New York.

Much is known about Ebeneezer Steele Peake, for within the Episcopal Church of Minnesota, he is considered one of the three great nineteenth century missionaries. In the summer of 1856, Father Peake and his bride had come out to Minnesota from New York, their intent being to minister to the native people at the St. Columba mission on Gull Lake. Under Father Peake's supervision, a school and a church were built. But this was not a good time for Yankee missionaries in northern Minnesota. A year earlier, the Ojibwe had ceded to the United States their rights to an enormous tract of land, extending from the St. Louis River in the Lake Superior watershed west to the Red River that separated Minnesota from Dakota, and from Lake Mille Lacs north some 150 miles across the entire Territory of Minnesota. All this they had given up for five cents an acre and the promise of goods that were slow in coming. So unfriendly was the Gull Lake environment that Ebeneezer Peake eventually turned the mission over to his Indian assistant, Deacon En-megah-bowh, and moved his family south to where the Crow Wing River met the Mississippi. This was the town of Crow Wing, until recently a village of traders and hunters, but now the new county seat of Crow Wing County in the new State of Minnesota. In 1859 Crow Wing gave promise of becoming the lumbering capital of the state. Although no sawmill had yet found its way this far north, the town could boast at least one frame home, a handful of log buildings, a Catholic church, a collection of lean-to whiskey shops, and a ring of wigwams marking the perimeter.

And what a bustling place it was. In season its rivers were jammed with rafts of logs from the great pine forests—virgin timber on its way downstream to St. Cloud and St. Anthony. The single road through town was the well-worn trader's trail from Fort Garry in Canada to St. Paul. Here the Red River ox cart trains often stopped to rest before the final trek south. These were the trains that defined and drove the commerce of Crow Wing. From time to time they could be heard from afar, the distinctive creaking of two to four hundred wooden wheels, for the ox cart was but a two-wheeled vehicle of wood and leather. On the way south, each cart overflowed with valuable pelts from the far north country. On the way north, the same carts were filled with manufactured goods of every kind. The placid oxen were kept in line by a driver on foot, perhaps one man to three carts. Once the ox carts came in sight, it was the drivers who commanded attention—"half-breeds, sons of the traders and hunters, looking more Indian than white . . . dressed in buckskin with bright colored knit sash about the waist and a coonskin cap with a tail hanging down behind or a broad brimmed hat."[3]

The arrival of the Red River ox carts at Crow Wing was always a time of celebration, for the drivers and their hangers-on brought not only business, but also a much-needed gaiety to this otherwise unpredictable and often dangerous environment.

And what a mix was the Crow Wing population—Indian men in "breach cloth and blanket" mixing with their own cousins dressed in Yankee hats and pants, traders, lumber entrepreneurs of every mix, including more than a few scoundrels, and daily new immigrants dragging in from the east with their wagons, covered and otherwise. These newcomers came to press their claims at the land registration office—claims to government lands that until recently had been home to the Mississippi bands.

Somewhere amongst the motley crowd would probably have been one Mr. Simeon Weaver, owner of a team of horses and a wagon, ready and willing to transport persons and goods to the Indian settlements or to government lands lying north and west. Sim Weaver, as he was known, presented himself as the "Indian expert" in Crow Wing. He had recently strengthened his reputation by marrying the Ojibwe woman Kah-goonce from Sandy Lake. The Weavers already had one small child, a boy, and they intended to have more. As a matter of fact, there was also another child, for Kah-goonce had come into the marriage with an Indian daughter, now age eleven.

We can presume that Father Peake may well have known the child Keche-ogemah from his time at the St. Columba mission. Probably Kah-goonce had occasionally brought the child to the mission. Perhaps the priest had recognized a certain spark in her, a potential to be developed. Perhaps Kah-goonce had looked up the priest after she moved to Crow Wing. Perhaps she had told him it was difficult now with a white husband who wished to establish his own family. Perhaps Father Peake already had ideas for the future of the child Keche-ogemah. He would wait and see.

For almost three years Ebeneezer Peake observed the Indian girl Keche-ogemah. No doubt he introduced the child to Bishop Henry Whipple of the Episcopal Church when he made his annual visits to the northern missions. Did the bishop also see in this adolescent girl a great potential, were she given the proper education? We shall never know. What we do know is that in the spring of 1862, when the United States was at war with the Confederacy, Father Peake and his family left Crow Wing, for he had joined the Wisconsin Volunteers as a chaplain in the Union Army. Before taking up his new duties, he delivered his wife and children to their temporary home in Faribault. He also delivered the Ojibwe girl Keche-ogemah to the home of Bishop Whipple and his wife Cornelia.

Isabel Beaupre, the Bishop's Ward

I had never known of an atheist among the North American Indians.
They believe unquestioningly in a future life. They believe that everything
in nature—the laughing waterfall, the rock, the sky, the forest—contains
a divinity, and all mysteries are accounted for by these spirits, which they
call manidos. . . . The Ojibwes are not idolaters, they never bow down nor
worship any created thing. They have preserved a tradition of one Supreme
God, whom they call "Kitche-manido"—the uncreated, or the kind,
cherishing Spirit. They believe that the Grand Medicine was given them by
an intermediate deity, the Grand Medicine God. . . . The Christian religion
is considered greatly inferior, as its promises are for the future life.
—Bishop Henry Whipple, 1899[4]

The Whipple household must have been a lively place in those years, for in addition to six Whipple children, there was always at least one Indian child about. Usually the girl or boy was of the Dakota tribe, for they were near neighbors to Faribault. Then, in 1862, the first Ojibwe child arrived—Keche-ogemah, fluent in two languages, knowing how to read and write, and in Cornelia Whipple's opinion, ripe for the kind of education every female child ought to have.

But first things first. Keche-ogemah had never been baptized. Thus, on the sixth of July 1862, shortly after the bishop returned home from dealing with serious troubles at the two Minnesota River Dakota Agencies, he baptized Keche-ogemah and gave her a pair of Christian names—Isabel Elizabeth. Henceforth she would be known as Isabel Beaupre. The transformation had begun.

As if Cornelia Whipple did not have enough on her hands, with her husband mostly away and a houseful of children underfoot, she conducted a girls' school within her home. The students included both children from the community and whatever Indian child might be under her care at the time. Isabel attended the school with its heavy emphasis on religion, but she also was required to learn about cooking and food preservation, about simple medicinal remedies, about sewing and mending, and above all about orderliness— everything a "civilized" household required. (Education in the Whipple household must have taken well with young Isabel. Decades later her Ojibwe grandchildren would recall visiting Grandmother's home at White Earth, having afternoon tea with a doily under the cream and sugar, and afterward Grandmother sweeping up cookie crumbs with a broom and dustpan.)

On September 20 of that year, Isabel celebrated her fifteenth birthday. Bishop Whipple, now her surrogate father, was hardly at home that fall, for that summer a bloody conflict had engulfed the width and breadth of southern Minnesota. (See, "Wars Within a War" below). Either he was off to Washington to plead with President Lincoln on behalf of 300 condemned Dakota prisoners, or he was at Fort Snelling comforting the more than 1,600 native men, women and children imprisoned outdoors at the fort, or up the Minnesota River valley comforting those of his white flock who had survived the killings. Yet Cornelia Whipple had taught the child well. When the bishop did return home for Isabel's examination, she was more than prepared. On December 7, at the Cathedral of our Merciful Savior in Faribault, Isabel Beaupre was confirmed and welcomed as an adult into the Christian fold. Her education likely did not stop with confirmation, for she continued to live in the Whipple household, a place where learning shared an equal place with virtue.

There is no record as to whether Isabel longed for her mother, for Sandy Lake, for the wilderness, or for Crow Wing. It would be seven years before the Whipples sent her back to her own people. In that time, their lives too had been transformed, for they were now on their way to a "civilized society" on the White Earth Ojibwe Reservation.

But how did it happen that the Ojibwe were being gathered together in this small part of their once vast domain? To answer this question, we must turn our attention to the broader issue of how the Euro-Americans arrived on the scene in the first place.

War & Peace

A Bundle of Treaties

The complicated and often tragic litany of treaties between the United States government and the various Ojibwe bands rests on foundations laid by President Thomas Jefferson in 1803, when the United States acquired from France some 828,000 square miles of land stretching from the Mississippi River west to the Rocky Mountains. The northern border of this vast land is today, with exceptions, the border between the United States and Canada. The very existence of the acquisition—known to us as the Louisiana Purchase—was unknown to the Ojibwe who dwelled at Pembina, Rainy Lake, Ottertail, and other villages west of the Mississippi River, yet it placed all of these villages and lands in the heartland of the United States of America.

From the beginning, the United States government sought to negotiate treaties with the tribes they came upon, offering money and goods, both at the time of signing and into some indefinite future, in return for title to the lands the native peoples had hitherto considered their home. In 1805 such a treaty was signed with Ojibwe chiefs from the Ohio River Valley, in 1826 with Ojibwe chiefs at the Fond du Lac village near Lake Superior, and in 1837 at Fort Snelling, where the Minnesota and Mississippi rivers meet.

These treaty events were accompanied by the exchange of gifts, and always a great deal of alcohol. Yet there was never unanimity among the Indian representatives. At the Fort Snelling negotiations, the Lake Superior bands were asked to cede to the

United States the mighty pine forests between the Mississippi and St. Croix rivers. Several of the leaders pointed out that some of the Mississippi bands who would be most affected by the treaty were not present or even represented. Never mind, the pressures were difficult to resist, and ultimately even the most resistant among Ojibwe leaders felt compelled to sign. (Descendants of headmen who participated in these early treaty negotiations remember even today who succumbed first to the wily negotiators and who resisted to the last.)

These negotiations were invariably conducted between the United States of America and the Chippewa Nation[*], as if the Ojibwe, wherever situated, were an identifiable entity. But after deposits of copper and iron were discovered on the north shore of Lake Superior, the government changed its tack, seeking to isolate the Ojibwe of this region in order to extract mineral rights to the rich deposits. By a treaty signed in 1842, the government succeeded in this, and the concept of two distinct groups emerged: the "Lake Superior Chippewa" and the "Chippewa of the Mississippi." The division turned out to be convenient for the Ojibwe themselves. To this day both individuals and bands identify with one or the other, especially in their dealings with the United States Government.

In 1847 the Lake Superior and Mississippi bands were summoned to a meeting at Fond du Lac, at the time a major community in the land of the Lake Superior bands. The United States Commissioner offered a proposal that at first glance appeared to be beneficial. These reservations would provide a buffer zone between the Ojibwe and the Dakota, something the Ojibwe desperately wanted. In those years, bands from the Dakota tribe presented a chronic threat, for they still coveted lands lost to the Ojibwe in earlier decades.

Just to the east, the Territory of Wisconsin was preparing to enter the Union as a state, hence presumably no place for an aboriginal people. The United States Commissioner proposed a plan by which the Ojibwe west of Wisconsin would cede to the

---

[*] "Chippewa" is a corruption of "Ojibwe" and will only be used here when it is part of a quotation or an organizational name.

Government a huge tract of land, what is today a large portion of central Minnesota. This land would be set aside as a reservation for the Menominee Tribe, which at the time occupied the great pine forests of Wisconsin. Likewise a reservation would be set aside for the Winnebago from Iowa, for they too were under pressure by white agricultural interests. The United States government intended to relocate these indigenous people north to the Ojibwe lands. It was not difficult to obtain the necessary signatures at Fond du Lac, so serious was the Dakota threat. What happened afterward, however, would mark the beginning of a deep-seated and permanent distrust among these northern bands, a distrust that still surfaces whenever the federal government comes bearing gifts.

As it turned out, the Menominee Tribe simply refused to leave its Wisconsin forests for a new and unfamiliar homeland. Some of the Winnebago did briefly relocate to the upper Mississippi reservation, but they soon returned to their old homeland as well. A year after the Treaty of Fond du Lac, the Minnesota Territory was created and the rush of economic opportunists commenced. Rather than returning the empty reservation land to the Ojibwe, the United States government divided the land, then offered it to lumbering interests while opening the agricultural lands to new settlers.

From this time on, "reservation" was the norm. It would only be a matter of time before what were once the realms of the Ojibwe and the Dakota would come under the complete jurisdiction of the United States. In 1851, at Traverse des Sioux, headwaters of the Minnesota River, the Dakota ceded most of southern Minnesota in exchange for a limited reservation along the Minnesota River and the promise of annual cash payments in gold over a period of fifty years. If ever there was a massive swindle associated with an Indian Treaty it was at Traverse des Sioux, but that would not become clear for another decade.

In 1854 and 1855, a number of treaties were negotiated with the Ojibwe. In return for cash, goods, and promises of education, the bands at Grand Portage, Fond du Lac, Mille Lacs, Sandy Lake, Rabbit Lake, Gull Lake, Cass Lake, and Pokegama gave up claims to most of northern Minnesota. All that was left to them were the mini-reservations surrounding their villages. For the moment, the Pembina, the Bois Fort, and the Red Lake bands had not yet been reigned in. Eventually, the Pembina and the Bois Fort would cede the entire fertile Red River Valley to the federal government for ten cents an acre.

The Red Lake Ojibwe never ceded all of their land to the United States. To this day, Upper and Lower Red Lake, together with the surrounding land, remain a distinctive feature on every Minnesota map.

Wars Within a War

Who is guilty of the causes which desolated our border? At whose door is the blood of these innocent victims? I believe that God will hold the nation guilty.
—Bishop Whipple, 1899[5]

The year was 1858. The State of Minnesota had just been admitted to the union, and its fledgling economy based on lumber, agriculture, and milling was burgeoning. Yet seven years after the fateful Treaty of Traverse des Sioux, the Dakota bands were in a state of despair, on the verge of starvation, and totally in debt to the traders on whom they were now dependent. Thus it was not difficult to persuade these Indian people to cede half of their already limited reservation in return for cash. As it turned out, virtually all of the money was paid directly to the traders to cover debts. With so much collusion between the Indian Agents and the traders, the figures were simply not to be trusted. A scenario for violence was slowly building.

Three years later the United States was at war with itself. Minnesota was the first to offer volunteers in the fight to preserve the union. By the time the bloody affair was over in 1865, 22,000

Minnesota volunteers, including a handful of Ojibwe and Dakota, had fought and died for the Union.

In early June of 1862, when little public attention was being paid to the dismal situation along the Minnesota River, several thousand Dakota gathered at the Indian Agency in anticipation of the annual payments due them in provisions and gold currency. The payments had not arrived. There were rumors they would never arrive, for the United States was involved in a great war for survival. The Dakota were hungry; they were destitute. The warehouses at the agency were full, but credit to the people had run out. For two months they camped outside the agency awaiting the promised distribution. Petitions to open the warehouses were routinely denied. After six weeks, a group of young warriors attempted to storm a warehouse. They were rebuffed by soldiers from Fort Ridgely. To assuage the people, Major Galbraith, the Indian Agent, attempted to deliver payment in paper money that, given the wartime inflation, was almost worthless. It was a clever idea, for once the gold was delivered, he could pocket the difference himself. But the Indian leaders refused to accept the paper even though starvation was already taking its toll. Finally, Galbraith did promise that payment in gold would be forthcoming, but it would take time.

For the Dakota, time had run out. On August 18, militant Dakota warriors mounted massive and deadly attacks on the white population all across the Minnesota River Valley. Chief Little Crow became their reluctant leader, but only after he made the case for peace.

> *We are only little herds of buffalo left scattered; the great herds that once covered the prairies are no more. See! The white men are like locusts when they fly so thick that the whole sky is a snowstorm. You may kill one—two—ten; yes, as many as the leaves in the forest yonder, and their brothers will not miss them. [If you] kill one—two—ten times ten, then ten times ten will come to kill you . . .*

When one of the warriors interrupted to call him a coward, the chief replied, "Taoyateduta* is not a coward. He will die with you."[6]

The Sioux Uprising, or Dakota Conflict, as it is now called, was the bloodiest Indian War in United States history. At least 350 white civilians were killed, in addition to a number of soldiers. The number of Dakota who died is probably far greater. Numbers were never recorded, but they include many besides the warriors themselves, for a great portion of the population—1,658 men, women, and children—was rounded up, taken to Fort Snelling by wagon, and over one wretched winter placed outside under guard in closely packed tipis. Not surprisingly, a measles epidemic broke out, taking its deadly toll, especially among the children. After that the Dakota were hounded out of Minnesota.

Far to the north, in the land of the Ojibwe, stood Fort Ripley on the Mississippi River, the United States outpost in Ojibwe country. On the very day of the first Dakota attack the commanding officer at Fort Ripley heard a rumor. Hole-in-the-Day,† Chief of the Gull Lake band, was plotting with Little Crow to foment a statewide uprising. The officer immediately sent soldiers to arrest Hole-in-the-Day. A brief gun battle ensued. The chief escaped with his followers into the wilds beyond the Gull Lake Reservation, but not before ransacking the land registry office at Crow Wing and the St. Columba Episcopal Mission at Gull Lake.

This brief skirmish has often been called "Hole-in-the-Day's War." It may well be the only war in history where there were no casualties.

Hole-in-the-Day's escapades were not in vain. The symbolism of his chosen targets—Christian proselytizing and land registration—was not lost on the missionaries nor on Minnesota's politicians. So shaken were they all that they rewarded the chief with a lifetime $1,000 cash annuity, at the same time increasing supplies to the destitute Gull Lake Reservation. Yet, the St. Columba mission remained, and the pressure on the Ojibwe to cede their lands only increased.

---

* Little Crow
† Que-we-zain-ce, Chief Hole-in-the-Day the Younger.

White Earth: The Grand Experiment

The stranger read the paper written by the White Father . . . On-da-bi-
tung said the paper meant that they must leave the rainy country and
move to a place called a Native Area. The new place would be theirs
forever. The Ojibwe would live in one part of the forest and the strangers
in another, and neither would go into the other's part.[7]
—*Night Flying Woman*, by Ignatia Broker

All across Minnesota the Euro-Americans had been made wary by the Dakota Conflict of 1862. With the Dakota a solution had been found—execute those presumed to be murderers and banish the rest as far as the Missouri River. With the Ojibwe, it was not so easy. Scattered here and there across the northern half of the state, ranging from "uncivilized" full-bloods to somewhat "integrated" mixed-bloods, the population could not easily be categorized. A solution was conceived that addressed this unique situation—*consolidation*. Nowadays the descriptive word might be "concentration." If this could be achieved, then all energies could focus on a grand experiment in social engineering. It would require cooperation between government and the private sector, with major input from the Christian churches. Education and religion would be the bywords. *For their own good, the Indians must be made into civilized members of the greater society!*

Negotiations to bring all this about commenced in 1863, with the Mississippi bands as first candidates. A year later, amid great expectations, they signed a treaty that exchanged existing reservation land for lands with presumably greater agricultural potential.

In these events Bishop Whipple played a prominent role as a voice for the state's native population. A year earlier, following the Dakota Conflict, he had intervened personally with President Abraham Lincoln on behalf of the Dakota. Some seven hundred Dakota men had been convicted of murder, rape, and other atrocities in a jury-rigged trial that allowed the defendants no legal counsel; 303 of the accused had been sentenced to death. The bishop claimed to know them all. He sat down with the president and went through the names, one by one, crossing out most of them. In the end thirty-eight were executed in a mass hanging at Mankato, the entire spectacle witnessed by the gathered townspeople.

Now the good bishop chose to intervene on behalf of the Ojibwe. The lands set aside for the Mississippi bands were not well suited for agriculture. The Indians deserved better than that. Thus a new location surrounding Rice Lake and White Earth Lake was

The White Earth Indian Agency, ca 1872
MHS photo by Hoard & Tenney

identified—thirty-six entire townships, almost 1,300 square miles. This huge tract of land, named for the light clay under the topsoil, would always carry the name *The White Earth Reservation*.

If ever a tract of land could be termed "bountiful," it was *White Earth*. In the eastern parts were the great pine forests, to the west rich agricultural land interspersed with lakes, rice marshes, and hardwood forests. As if this were not enough, the government promised all kinds of assistance, including a sawmill, houses, financial support for farm implements, breeding stock, schools, medical care, and annual payments! Surely it was an offer that leaders of the Mississippi Ojibwe could hardly refuse.

Thus, in 1867, ten chiefs from the Mississippi bands, including Hole-in-the-Day, were invited to Washington, D.C., to negotiate this new and more favorable treaty. The treaty included all that was promised beforehand, plus up to 160-acre allotments of land to full-blood Ojibwe, and also to mixed-bloods so long as they lived on the reservation. For the first time, a distinction was made between mixed-bloods who lived on the reservation and those who did not, a distinction that continues to be of great importance, as well as a bone of contention, in this 21st century.

And what did the Mississippi bands give up for all this? Great stands of timber, already coveted and routinely poached upon by the lumbering interests of the state. The ties between lumber and politics would later become a scandal, too late, however, for the tribe whose lands, by treaty, had been ceded for almost nothing to the United States of America.

The 1868 Removal

My poor people have gone away brokenhearted.
—Father En-megah-bowh
of the Gull Lake Mission

What a curious term is "removal," yet it was the accepted term for the great migration that now commenced. As it was to turn out in later years, the term was more than accurate.

At first there was great reluctance to make the grand move. Above all, Hole-in-the-Day was not happy with the arrangements. He demanded that the government build houses for the people, to be ready when they arrived. He boasted that he would travel once more to Washington and renegotiate the treaty terms. But over his objections, two hundred Ojibwe full-bloods left Gull Lake for White Earth on June 4, 1868.

There must have been some high hopes among the travelers, for Chief Na-bun-ash-kong led the procession. He wore his head feathers and sang his war song all along the way. Certainly the journey was not without anxiety, for there were fears of the hostile Dakota, who still turned up in this part of Minnesota. Thus the Ojibwe marched beside their ox carts with guns loaded. On June 14, these first settlers arrived at their new homeland, encamping near the present town of White Earth. No one denied that a beautiful land lay before them. Their disappointment was in the discovery that the promised houses and sawmill were nowhere to be seen. The Indian people pitched their summer tipis, then began the laborious task of cutting and stacking logs for new homes, the promised sawmill, and an Episcopal church. Perhaps it would eventually all turn out for the better.

A few of the new arrivals soon drifted back to Gull Lake, bringing news that the government promises had not been met. Hole-in-the-Day felt vindicated. Now *he* would be their savior by renegotiating the treaty. One August day he set off in a horse and buggy for Crow Wing, his intention being to travel once again to Washington and meet with the United States government. It never came to that. Just outside Crow Wing, Hole-in-the-Day was ambushed. Later that day his bullet-ridden body was discovered in a ditch. The horse and buggy were nowhere to be found.* Such were the beginnings of the White Earth Ojibwe Reservation.

---

* Who killed Hole-in-the-Day has never been confirmed.

Crossed Roots

Thus, in 1869 when Isabel Beaupre, once Keche-ogemah, was sent by the Whipples to join other Ojibwe at White Earth, she was participating in a social experiment being played out on a grand scale across the entire American frontier. She had not been at White Earth long before she met Fred Peake. He would soon join her in facing the challenges of a more modest social experiment—that of raising a family.

The Brothers Peake

One might suppose that Ebeneezer Peake had some matchmaking in mind when he took the fourteen-year-old Keche-ogemah from her family and delivered her into the household of Bishop Whipple. Not long after he had moved to Crow Wing, Ebeneezer's four brothers, Charles, Giles, George, and Frederick, came out from New York to join him. No doubt they were encouraged by the promise of immense opportunities for any man with a bit of ambition.

One might ask whence came these bold Peake men so intent on seeking their fortunes in the wilderness? Indeed, much has been documented, at least on the male side. It begins with one Christopher Peake, who was born in England in about 1612. He emigrated to the Massachusetts colony and married one Dorcas French, also from England. This marriage begat Jonathan, whose marriage begat Christopher, whose marriage begat another Christopher, whose marriage begat Moses, who fought in the American Revolution and whose marriage begat Oliver, whose marriage begat William, whose marriage begat eleven children, including Ebeneezer, Charles, Giles, George, and Frederick.

Among the descendents of the five brothers there were always rumors of an Indian grandmother from the Choptank tribe in Delaware, for the Peake brothers were not only known to be better looking than the average Yankee, but also a shade darker.

The five Peake brothers: Standing, left to right,
Frederick, Sr. & Ebeneezer, ca 1875

Of Charles, Giles, George, and Frederick little is known today beyond citations in Becker County records and fragment memoirs of their contemporaries, those white entrepreneurs who came out to northern Minnesota where opportunity was there for the taking. *1858:* Eighteen-year-old Frederick Peake, in partnership with one Joseph Wakefield, opened a trading store at Crow Wing. *1861-1865:* Four of the Peake brothers enlisted in the Civil War. Ebeneezer served as chaplain to the Wisconsin Volunteers. Charles, Giles, and George, along with a number of Ojibwe mixed-bloods, served in the Minnesota Volunteers. *1867:* Frederick Peake traveled to Washington, D.C., during negotiations regarding the treaty that created the White Earth Reservation. No doubt Frederick was soliciting government contracts. *1867-1868:* Frederick Peake's efforts were not in vain. That winter he took a crew of Crow Wing men to White Earth Lake, where they cut and banked a quantity of pine logs along the shore. When the work was completed, they all returned to Crow Wing. The logs were to be used in the building of the promised White Earth sawmill, a major feature of the 1867 treaty. The mill was to be built in the spring of 1868, before the great migration commenced. Like so many other government promises, this promise was not kept. *1868:* Early that spring, a party of five left Crow Wing with horses and plows, to break the first land at White Earth. They too were under contract with the United States government. The party included Frederick Peake, who remained at White Earth. Later that summer, he opened the first store on the White Earth Reservation. *1869:* Charley Peake had a trading store at Otter Tail Lake, with nothing to trade but fish and potatoes. Giles also was at Otter Tail Lake. Both Giles and Charles married Ojibwe women and remained in the area. Ebeneezer had already moved on to missions far beyond Minnesota.[8]

But it is Frederick Peake who is about to capture our attention. In Ebeneezer's mind, brother Frederick, the youngest, gave the greatest promise of success. Likewise, Ebeneezer must have seen in the Indian girl Keche-ogemah a similar potential. All she needed was the training promised in such a civilized household as that of Bishop Whipple. So must Ebeneezer have reasoned.

Why the delay in Isabel's return to the north? Perhaps the Whipples earlier viewed the country as too wild for such a girl as Isabel. But now, in 1869, it was time for Isabel to go back to Crow Wing. Nor is it difficult to imagine how young Frederick and Isabel met. Surely En-megah-bowh, now an Episcopalian priest, remembered Keche-ogemah from her childhood years at Sandy Lake. Likewise, he was certainly well acquainted with all of the Peake brothers.

Frederick Peake and Isabel Beaupre were married at Crow Wing in 1870. The following year, their first child, Frederick W. Peake, Jr.—Fred—arrived. Altogether, six children would be born to this marriage: Frederick W., Jr., David E., Emily E., Charles H., Henry B., and George C. All six would be enrolled members of the White Earth Reservation, for Isabel indeed was from Sandy Lake, one of the Mississippi bands for which White Earth was designed.

The year of Fred Jr.'s birth, 1871, was a banner year for northern Minnesota. That year the Northern Pacific railroad reached Becker County from Minneapolis and then cut across from Brainerd all the way to Fargo in the Dakota Territory. Along the railroad line from Minneapolis to Fargo, just south of the White Earth Reservation, a new town—*Detroit**—appeared.

Frederick Peake was not about to let opportunity pass him by. In the spring of 1872, when Detroit was not yet a year old, he moved his family to the new town. There he and brother Giles opened a store. One must presume it was successful, for shortly thereafter, and not without controversy, Detroit became the county seat of Becker County as well as a major railroad depot. The Peake children attended public school and the family attended the local Episcopal church.

For a moment they might well have forgotten their mixed-blood status, but in 1882 tragedy struck. Frederick Peake died. How Isabel and her six young children managed for the next eight years we shall never know. What we do know is that when it came to mothering, Isabel Peake had no equal.

---

* In 1926 Detroit, Minnesota, was renamed Detroit Lakes.[9]

The Nelson Act

In 1890 Isabel Peake married one Fred Schneider, a recent arrival from Pennsylvania. The following year the couple acquired 160 lakeside acres of allotted land, built a substantial house, and began farming, all within the White Earth Reservation. They even had the privilege of naming the little lake *Snyder Lake*. It is still on the map, as Snider Lake.

Now how did this fortunate development all come about? In fact, it was the result of the Nelson Act "for the relief and

**Isabel (Peake) Schneider, Fred Schneider,
& three Peake sons, Snyder Lake ca 1900.**

civilization of the Chippewa of Minnesota," as passed by the United States Congress in 1889. This act provided for the implementation of a more general congressional act passed two years earlier. That was the Dawes Act, which permitted the allotment to individual Indian *people* of lands that by treaty had been previously set aside for Indian *tribes*.

For several years there had been intense pressure by Minnesota lumber and agricultural constituencies to wrest from tribal control at least some of the vast White Earth pine stands, as well as the rich prairie expanses. From their point of view, these lands were greatly underused. The White Earth Reservation alone comprised more than 800,000 acres, yet harbored a population of just 3,000 Indian people. Why should any group need so much space? So ran the arguments. Thus, following an interminable investigation undertaken by a special presidential commission, innumerable meetings with Indian leaders, and expansive promises that later turned out to be words of a "forked tongue," Congress passed the Nelson Act, named for its principal sponsor, Minnesota's Senator Knut Nelson. For those members of the Mississippi bands who had migrated to White Earth before 1870, the Nelson Act provided allotments of 80 acres to each adult, the expectation being that they would all turn to farming. In the hope of attracting members of other Ojibwe bands to White Earth, they too were offered allotments, though of smaller size. The Nelson Act also included government-supported agricultural assistance and forbade the selling of allotted land without the approval of the Secretary of the Interior, all to protect a people presumed to be backward and naive.

Other provisions in the act were not so favorable. The tribe was forced to open up for public sale a wide strip of forest land on the eastern border of the reservation. It was assumed the Indian people themselves, principally the business-savvy French-Indian mixed-bloods, would have equal access in the bidding process, but that was not to be. The outside lumber interests had it all sewed up before the bidding began. Still the tribe retained ownership of the remaining timberlands, presumably to generate profit to the tribe as a whole. All in all, the Nelson Act appeared to be a mixed bag.

If one were to be cynical about the initial impact of this allotment process, one might refer to Isabel Peake, now Schneider, as a "land squaw."* Following the implementation of the Nelson Act, more than a few non-Indian men courted and married Ojibwe

---

*Squaw: an absolutely demeaning word for an Indian woman, with its roots in the Iroquois language.

women, added their names to their wives' deeds, then after a decent time sold the land and fled the marriage. Surely one might have questioned the marriage of Fred Schneider to Isabel Peake just months before she took her allotment. But as it turned out, their marriage was lifelong and their home at Snyder Lake a place of noted hospitality to Isabel's widely extended family. This marriage produced two children, one of whom died in infancy, and ended only with Isabel's death in 1929.

Frederick W. Peake, Jr.

Emily's father Fred (1871-1935)

It is with a mother's hopeful heart that I write these words, asking you to send me an immediate reply whether my beloved son, F. W. Peake is improving any. Do not hesitate to tell me his condition. Have you strong belief of his recovery? I am very grateful for the care and consideration that my dear son is receiving at the hands of the Great Government's skillful medical men.
—Letter from Isabel Schneider, formerly Isabel Peake, to St. Elizabeth Hospital, November 22, 1899

Isabel, like her mentor Cornelia Whipple, valued learning above all. There can be no doubt that after her husband's death, her older children left school to help support the family. Anticipating her remarriage and using whatever clout she could muster, Isabel succeeded at last in enrolling two of the children at the Indian Industrial School in Carlisle, Pennsylvania. Thus, in the fall of 1890 Fred and Emily, ages nineteen and seventeen, were sent off by train to Carlisle.

Theoretically, every Indian child in the United States had access to the Carlisle School, a boarding school owned by the federal government and operated under military supervision. The school was to be the instrument of their transformation into useful, productive citizens, never mind that it would be decades before the United States Congress granted full-bloods U.S. citizenship. The Carlisle School operated under strict discipline. The hair of both boys and girls was shorn immediately on arrival; their native language was suppressed and their native religion banned. All this

Graduating Class, 1892; Indian Industrial School, Carlisle, PA, Fred Peake, Jr. first row on the right

was to be replaced by a Christian culture and a rigid academic education plus acquisition of skills appropriate to a household, to agricultural pursuits, and to an industrial society.

For those who came from traditional Indian families, Carlisle must initially have been an experience from hell. But to the mixed-blood Peakes from Minnesota, this was the beginning of opportunity. Some twenty years later, Fred Peake would write an unsolicited tribute to his alma mater:

> *I have not been in touch with the Carlisle School for some time, yet at heart I feel deeply interested in the great school. It is the greatest factor in the emancipation of the Indians. It has given a part of the race a great start for assimilation and citizenship in the American Government. I wish Carlisle great success.*[10]

We do know that Fred succeeded very well in his two years at Carlisle. Already in his first year he was a member of the winning debate team and in his second year served with two faculty members as judge of the annual intramural debate event. The subject: "Resolved that the elective franchise should be extended to women." The three-member judging panel determined that each speaker "acquitted himself with credit," and that the affirmative side prevailed. That year, 1892, Fred Peake graduated and entered the Dickinson Preparatory School in nearby Philadelphia. He was determined to be a lawyer!

Dead and Down

The records of White Earth Indian exploitation by unscrupulous white men, some of them prominent citizens and businessmen, aided by their hired mixed-blood agents, constitute some of the blackest pages in the history of the American Indian.
— Federal Indian Commissioner, 1920[11]

Looking back on the sometimes hopeful, yet often tragic, history of White Earth, one is led very quickly to the Nelson Act and the so-called Dead and Down Act, both passed by Congress in the year 1889. The Nelson Act, among other things, provided for the ceding and sale of four entire townships of White Earth prime timberland. The Dead and Down Act permitted the president to grant permits to Indians to cut and sell "dead and down" timber on reservations so long as the proceeds went to the Indians themselves. These twin developments marked the beginning of a tragedy that would forever be known as the "timber scandal."

But it didn't end there. In 1897 an Amendment to the Dawes Act provided that Indians could cut dead and down timber from lands that had already been ceded. Whatever Congress's intention might have been, the illegal cutting of timber on trust lands began in earnest, resulting in the total scalping of these virgin forests. So great was the public outcry that the Dead and Down Act was suspended in 1899, too late for the great northern Minnesota forests and too late for Fred Peake.

Fred had been involved in timber transactions on behalf of the tribe. In time the injustices occasioned by the bizarre statutes and the exploitative atmosphere of the times took their toll on the young man's psyche. In the fall of 1899, Fred was sent by his tribe to St. Elizabeth's Hospital for the Insane in Washington, D.C. There the diagnosis was "acute mania."

How all this came about is best told by his mother Isabel. Presented here are four letters, three written by Isabel and one by the U.S. Assistant Commissioner of Indian Affairs.[12]

White Earth Reservation, December 4th, 1899
A. B. Richardson, M.Ed.
Supt. Gov't. Hospital for the Insane
St. Elizabeth, D.C.

Dear Sir:

With a grateful heart I read your kind letter concerning my dear afflicted son. It brought great healing to my sore heart. My tribe as well as all my family are very thankful & trust your medical white men in skillful treatment.

From infancy my dear son seemed doomed to a fate of great injustice from every side. His own father never treated him as a parent should. Since into manhood he has met with the same injustice & great opposition in every business he undertook to transact. He graduated in Carlisle Penn. under Capt. R.W. Pratt.* Then entered the Dickinson Law College, paying his own expenses, earning the money by hard labor among the Eastern

---

* Founder of the Carlisle Indian Industrial School.

farmers during vacations. His health being not in a state any longer to earn more money by hand labor he returned home without being admitted to the Bar. Requiring six months more study.

Immediately upon his arrival here, my people, the Chippewas, earnestly requested him to look after our affairs with the U.S. government, which he did. After two years of mental labor, anxiety, meeting all his own expense, his work was all overturned by Commissioner Browning and Maj. Allen, Indian Agent of this Reservation at that time, these persons working in harmony with the Pine Ring of Minnesota. His funds again exhausted, he told the Indians to wait for a new administration & in the meantime go away & earn more money to work with. After this announcement, he set out for Washington State, doing business in Coeurdalene City & Walla Walla & Spokane, there again met with money losses, also a severe Rail Road accident, which nearly caused amputation of the right arm at the shoulder. Had it not been for the skillful care of the Rail Road Physicians the arm would have been lost.

His work for the Tribe began in '93. While [he was] out West, the tribe summoned him twice to return to them & appear before Congress as their Representative. Both times he and the tribe have been defeated by U.S. Agents & their associates who rule our Reservations as Monarchies. My dear son respects & loves law & cannot—or could not—withstand such despotism any longer. This is the cause of his Insanity.

The 25th of Sept. 1899 he closed his general counsel [office] on the White Earth Reservation. The Agent here refused to sign his [timber] contracts before a vast multitude of people. [The Agent] would not recognize the demands of the tribe. Then my dear son proceeded to another place, called the Leech Lake Pillager reservation where the Agent of several different bands of Chippewas promised to sign his contracts. But here he was deceived & insulted again. Very near the Reservation stands a Rail Road Town called Walker. Here he met Representative Eddy* &

---

* Frank M. Eddy, Congressman from Minnesota.

others & held a very hot argument against one another. This took place about the 26th or 27th of Sept.

Then the white people of that town (Walker) took him & put him in their jail. The Indians then became aware what took place & they immediately had their Agent go & set him free. Then they perceived some strange actions about him. The Agent told him to come home & take a rest. On the 1st of Oct. I was notified that he was insane, the word coming from Detroit, Minn., another Rail Road Town. There my husband & I found him in a miserable unhealthy place, what the white people call a Lockup. I could hardly recognize my precious boy, his pants & coat besmirched with blood. I think there was foul play also at some place, either at Walker or some Rail Road Station.

I do not wish Wm. T. Campbell* to be allowed to see my son. This person, who has been in Washington some three years, was sent by the Pine Syndicates, [who] call him the Minnesota Chippewa Representative. There is another person from this place who now resides in your City. I do not wish to have him in any conversation with, or see my boy. He is the person the people call Rev. J.A. Gilfillan.† This person & his followers fought against my darling boy's work with all the power they could command. They did not want the Indians taught anything regarding the Constitution of the United Sates or Citizenship. I think it would irritate my boy to see these persons.

The mixed-bloods that are partly rich & work with the Pine Ring have been telling the Indians for the last three & four years that my dear son was insane. Yet every class of people that knows my boy never thought or believed such a thing. Ah! It is very strange & bitter to me that their prediction should become true.

---

* William T. Campbell, interpreter with the 1899 White Earth Delegation to Washington, D.C.

† The Rev. Joseph A. Gilfillan, head of the Episcopal Mission at White Earth, where the Rev. En-megah-bowh was priest. Later, En-megah-bowh was relieved of his duties for reasons unknown.

I will send you, dear Sir, some of my precious boy's work as an Attorney for my tribe. The same papers the U.S. Indian Agents refused to sign when the majority of the tribe had elected my boy as their Representative. Do these papers indicate as being prepared by an unsound mind? This was his work done on the 16th, 17th & 18th of Sept. last. I hope my letter may not be irksome to you.

Perhaps you know not that in a far-off Indian Land daily Devotion from many a red man goes up to the Great Giver of life, to bless & strengthen the wisdom of the white medicine men & cure our loved one.

Please return the papers when convenient. Hope to hear soon from you. My children's father, a white man from Johnstown, N.Y., has been dead ten years. I bear a different name now by a second marriage. I am a Chippewa Indian of Minnesota.

Very Respectfully, Isabel Schneider

White Earth, Jan. 22nd, 1900
F. W. Peake c/o A.B. Richardson, M.Ed.
St. Elizabeth Hospital, D.C.

My beloved Son,

I write to tell you that father & all your sisters are well. Emily[*] was home a little while this winter. Your brother Charles intends to come home next summer. Father cut a hole in the ice on the lake today. He & little sister Viola fished with hooks & lines and had fun enjoying this fine day. We have had very fine weather here this winter. There is no snow, but there is ice on the lakes. Now my dear son, will you write to me, your mother who has always loved

---

[*] Fred's married sister Emily Robitaille, having graduated from Carlisle and having received a teaching certtificate from Winona Normal School, was teaching in Minnesota.

you? Write & tell me how you feel. Would you like to have me send you some wild rice? I think the Doctor would have it cooked or soaked in beef soup, same as I made it at home for you. Write & tell me what to do about sending the rice.

We all send love & will be happy to hear from you. Will you tell the Doctor if you want me to come & see you?

My dear Son, I remain your loving Mother, Isabel Schneider

White Earth, March 7th, 1900
To A.B. Richardson, M.Ed.

Dear Sir:

I would be very thankful and pleased to receive a letter from you, or any of your assistants at least once a month about my dear afflicted son. I have received two letters from him personally. They are very dear to my heart, being that his own loved hands wrote them although they are not what a sane person would write. But I think he has improved considerably. He has not answered my last letter and I am very anxious to know why. Does receiving & writing letters renew his excitement too much? Are the Patients (those that can write) required to furnish their own stationery? If so, please let me know.

I do think that my dear son should not remain at the Gov't. Hospital as a Charity Charge. Our tribe has a Treasury at the Capitol out of which the Indian Department should be willing to grant my dear son compensation for his labours. I would not need to ask my tribe the second time to sign any legal documents to that purpose. I think that every person who believes in God & Justice would think it right that my dear son's money be returned, at least at the request of the tribe.

Hoping to hear from you soon about my boy, I am very Respectfully yours,

Isabel Schneider

Department of the Interior
Office of Indian Affairs
Washington, July 19th, 1900
A.B. Richardson, M.D.
Supt. Government Hospital for the Insane
Washington, D.C.

Sir:

I have your letter of the 8th instant, in which you report that F.W. Peake, a Chippewa Indian who was transferred to your Institution on October 1st, 1899, for medical treatment, from the White Earth Agency, Minnesota, has recovered and is in a fit condition to be discharged from your Asylum. You further recommend that he be furnished transportation to enable him to return to his home.

In reply I have to request that you have the said F.W. Peake report to this office, when transportation will be furnished him.

Very respectfully,

(signed) A.C. Tonner, Assistant Commissioner

Attorney Fred Peake

F.W. Peake, the big and good-looking Ogema lawyer, was a visitor in the
village last Friday, being here on business at the First State Bank.
—*Waubun Forum*, December 20, 1907

Fred Peake did indeed return home seemingly freed of his psychosis, at least for the time being. He was now twenty-nine years old and a young man in a hurry. Fred enrolled at the North Dakota College of Law in Grand Forks, received whatever degree they offered, and was admitted to the Minnesota Bar. He may well have been the first Indian lawyer in the State of Minnesota.

For the Indian people at White Earth, the first years of the new century were not good years. It was bad enough that their great pine forests had been virtually destroyed by the Nelson Act and its sequel, the Dead and Down Act. Then in 1902 Congress passed a seemingly innocuous law allowing Indians to sell *inherited* allotments—"dead Indian lands," as they came to be known—to non-Indians. A rider was added in 1904 permitting the Indians to sell the *timber* on their allotted lands to non-Indians. The final blow was in 1906. It was called the Clapp Amendment, and it removed all restrictions to the sale of allotted lands by both mixed-blood and full-blood adults.*

In the blink of an eyelash, thousands of acres were picked up at ridiculously low prices by speculators ranging from individual entrepreneurs to national syndicates. The Saint Paul & Pacific Railroad† was among those buying enough of the previously protected allotment land to build a railroad through the reservation and establish five new railroad towns. When the buying frenzy was over, between the lost timberlands and the lost agricultural lands, eighty percent of the White Earth Ojibwe Reservation was in other than Indian or tribal hands.

> *I remember it was 1906. The land sharks around here got land any way they could. My mother told me how she put down her thumbprint on a piece of paper. She couldn't write. She couldn't speak English. She was a full blood. She wasn't supposed to be able to sell her land, according to the law. People didn't know what they were putting their thumbprints down for. Some thought they were just renting their land.*
>
> Josephine Robinson, White Earth, undated.[13]

---

* Full-bloods presumably needed approval of the U.S. Secretary of the Interior, but that proved to be no barrier.
† In 1879 the railroad was bought up by J.J. Hill and made part of his Great Northern Railway, which eventually reached to the Pacific Ocean.

Later historians would refer to this outcome as the genesis of the "White Earth Tragedy." [14]

One of the towns the Great Northern created on the reservation was Ogema, founded in 1907. Fred Peake promptly set up his law practice in partnership—Fargo* and Peake, Attorneys at Law. Fred became Ogema's first mayor. Clearly there ought to be plenty of business now for Fargo and Peake.

Attorney Fred Peake, Ogema, ca 1907

---

* George K. Fargo, probably a grandson of William George Fargo (1818-1881), after whom Fargo, North Dakota, was named. William George Fargo was director and financial backer of the Great Northern Railroad, also a founder of the Wells-Fargo Express Company.

A Marriage of
North & South

We have traced the lineage of Emily Peake's family on her father's side from the era of treaties and the creation of the reservations down to the twenteith century. It remains for us to examine Emily's roots on her mother's side of the family.

Caroline Le Havre, the Creole

Emily Peake's Maternal Grandmother (1844-1926),
daughter of an Indian orphan

Grandma Carrie was quite small, under five feet, dark-skinned with dark eyes and black hair pulled back in a pug. She talked English very well, but couldn't pronounce her R's. Everybody liked her. She was always so polite and so accommodating, especially with little children. I remember Grandma in a big checkered apron, always cooking or sewing. Such a cheerful person she was.

—Emily Peake, undated

We are told that back in 1828, when Texas was but a province of Mexico, one Robert Le Havre, a Creole, set out from Louisiana on horseback in hopes of establishing a new life in Texas. Probably he had heard about the DeWitt Colony, a successful "American" experiment in the midst of this vast Mexican landscape. In 1825 Green DeWitt had organized a colonization society composed of

43

Missourians. He negotiated a land grant of several thousand acres from the Mexican government, on which he established a handful of American communities, including the town of Gonzalas,* where the Guadeloupe and San Marcos rivers meet.

Young Robert traveled west across the Sabine River as far as Gonzales. He settled down briefly in the hope of becoming a bona fide DeWitt colonist. He even anglicized his name to fit—Robert Harvey. But it was not to be. After two years of work with the colony, Robert was still unable to wrest a land grant for himself. One can postulate why he might have been rejected—perhaps his mixed ancestry or his deep-south origins, perhaps the fact that he had brought with him neither money nor a wife, but only a horse and a rifle. What we do know is that the young man was forced to make his way back home. En route to the border he encountered the smoldering ruins of an Indian village.† As the story goes, the village had recently been sacked by bandits and all of its inhabitants massacred—all, that is, except one. Robert found a child sitting among the ruins, a little girl who spoke Spanish. He scooped her up, continued on horseback to Louisiana, and deposited her at the home of his mother. Robert returned to Texas, this time to Nacogdoches. He was killed in a battle between Texas irregulars and Mexican uniformed cavalry, an event that foretold the coming war for Texas Independence. The date: August 2, 1832.

We know little of the Indian child's growing-up years except that the French language very quickly replaced her native Spanish. How long she remained with Robert's mother or where she went from there is unknown. All we know is that she took the family name of her rescuer—Le Havre. In 1844 a daughter was born to her—

---

* In October of 1835, Gonzales would be the site of the first battle in the war of Texas Independence. The following spring, thirty-two of the Town's citizens would answer the call of the besieged Alamo. All would be killed at the Alamo, their sacrifice not in vain. For later in that year Texas would declare itself an independent nation on its way to joining the United States of America.

† In 1892, the town of Genoa was founded on the site of this village. Today it is a Houston suburb on the southeast perimeter of the metro area.

Caroline Le Havre. Clearly this mother instilled in this daughter the pride and responsibilities associated with her adopted French culture. Over an entire lifetime, Caroline would keep not only her French accent, but also her attachment to French *style*. Likewise, she would speak of Robert as her father though he had died years before she was born. As to that Spanish Indian orphan turned French Creole, one suspects she died early. By 1860 Caroline was living in Attala County, Mississippi, near Choctaw Indian land.

Private Jim Beaupre, a Union Soldier

Emily Peake's maternal grandfather (1845-1908),
son of Joe Beaupre and his Ojibwe wife Josette

All that tragedy, all the killing, all that blood soaking into the earth, that
of red men, black men, white men—all that too is part of [Mississippi]
...We're not the only ones who've got blood guilt on us, got what the
preachers call sin; it's something to do with being a human, being a man,
something to do with the condition of the human race.
—Wyatt Cooper*

When the great American Civil War commenced in 1861, Minnesota was among the first states to offer troops. Was this not indeed a fight for freedom and nationhood? So inspired was Governor Alexander Ramsey that he sent recruiters out all across the state to solicit willing volunteers for the noble endeavor. Nor were the Indian reservations immune to the recruiter's zeal. There was a curious footnote in federal law, a footnote that may have been quite overlooked when it came to Ojibwe volunteers. Mixed-blood Indian men were to be eagerly sought out while full-bloods were

---

* Wyatt Cooper, 1927-1978, just one of the long list of famous twentieth century writers from Mississippi. (See Bibliography.)

to be rejected. As it turned out, the Ojibwe reservations of northern Minnesota yielded more volunteers per capita than most other areas of the state. The exact number is lost to history, yet a 1910 reunion of the surviving White Earth Civil War veterans suggests that at least as many Ojibwe full-bloods as mixed-bloods served with the Minnesota Volunteers. Missing from the 1910 reunion was one James Beaupre, also a resident of White Earth. He had died two years earlier.

But back to 1862, when Minnesota's Company G of the Fifth Regiment set out on its glorious mission. Jim Beaupre, second son of the Frenchman Joe Beaupre and his Ojibwe wife Josette,* answered the recruiter's call. By horseback, by wagon, and by stagecoach, he and other volunteers from the Pembina band made their way from the far north down to Fort Snelling. They were sworn in, provided with a uniform and rifle, given a bit of training, and in early May sent south to Corinth in Mississippi.

Jim Beaupre's battle experiences began quite dramatically at the end of May as Minnesota's Fifth Regiment joined in the Siege of Corinth. There were victories along the way, also defeats, as well as skirmishes that ended in a draw. Routinely these encounters, whether skirmishes or full-fledged battles, resulted in massive casualties on both sides. Private Jim was one of the lucky ones, on the move throughout the spring of 1863—from Corinth to Tuscumia in Alabama, back to Mississippi, then into Tennessee, south to Mississippi Springs and the Siege of Vicksburg. Company G's role at Vicksburg was to isolate the town from Jackson by guarding the railroad bridge across the Big Black River. After 47 days of siege, with the Vicksburg population literally starved out, the city fell to Union troops. On July 4, the day of surrender, Private Jim Beaupre was there. Then it was back to northern Mississippi, again into Tennessee, back to Vicksburg and Meridian, again at the Big Black River bridge, more skirmishes in the villages and countryside, north again into Tennessee, and back again to Vicksburg. All this in the two years since Jim Beaupre had arrived in the war-torn land of black and white that was Mississippi.

---

* Kah-ge-way gwon-nay-be-quay, Josette's Ojibwe name.

Years later, Caroline would insist she had met her husband Jim at Multona Springs* in central Mississippi, where she was taking the waters, so to speak. And just by chance, Private Jim Beaupre of Company G was also at Multona Springs, on vacation. The tale was hardly believable to Carrie's children, and certainly not to her grandchildren, but in fact this is probably what did occur. In June of 1864, members of the Fifth Regiment—all those who had reenlisted in the field—were given a two-month furlough. What could a mixed-blood from northern Minnesota do with a sixty-day furlough? To travel north to his home was clearly out of the question. Instead Jim Beaupre chose nearby Multona Springs, now occupied by Union forces. Here was a watering place in the heart of Choctaw Indian land—or rather, the remnant of land left after the tribe's 1832 surrender to the United States. One might suppose that Multona Springs was an oasis in the midst of a war-torn and racially divided South—a place for mixed-bloods of every sort.

Thus one can easily imagine Jim Beaupre, the French-Indian from Minnesota, taking note of Caroline Le Havre, the dark-skinned French-speaking young woman of seemingly very mixed roots. Future plans must have been made at Multona Springs. Still the war was far from finished. In August Private Jim rejoined Company G at Oxford, Mississippi, for nine more months of fighting—into Arkansas, even north into Missouri, east for the Battle of Nashville, back to Mississippi, and finally into Alabama.

On April 9, 1865, the Confederacy surrendered. The Fifth Regiment of the Minnesota Volunteers still had five months to serve. Company G was assigned to Demopolis, Alabama, until September 6, when Jim and the entire Fifth Regiment were discharged. Four days later, he and Caroline Le Havre were married by a southern judge. When and how Carrie had found her way to Jim's side in those chaotic times we shall never know. Their courtship is the stuff of fiction, which this tale is not.

---

* Multona Springs lay north of Ethel and west of McCool. The town has long since vanished.

Southern War Bride

Jim Beaupre, Ojibwe mixed-blood,
and Caroline Le Havre, Creole

On Tuesday afternoon at his home occurred the death of James Beaupre,
aged 63 years. He was a veteran of the Civil War, serving three years as a
member of Company G, Fifth Minnesota Volunteers. The deceased was an
invalid for several years but bore up with remarkable patience awaiting his
master's call. He was a man of fine character, of a kindly disposition and
had a host of friends both in this little village and at Wabasha, Minn.,
where he formerly resided. He is survived by his wife, three daughters . . .
and a son . . .
—The Tomahawk,* White Earth, March 10, 1908

Together the newlyweds made their way by riverboat up the
Mississippi as far as Wabasha, Minnesota. There they would make
their home. At Wabasha Carrie and Jim became the "Indian family"
in town. Never mind that a decade before the War this was the
village of Chief Wabasha, one of the greatest Dakota headmen.
By the time the Beaupres arrived, the Dakota had been banished
from the state. The remnant of Chief Wabasha's band was huddled
upstream along the river on a bit of land known as Prairie Island.
The town of Wabasha was now a major point of debarkation for
European immigrants, the southernmost river harbor for those
seeking a new home in Minnesota.

Over the years Caroline gave birth to ten children in Wabasha,
including daughter Louise, born in 1886. From Wabasha the
Beaupres sent at least two of their children off to Haskell Indian

---

* *The Tomahawk*, founded by Gus Beaulieu, was published at White Earth from
1903 to 1923.

Institute in Kansas. Rightly or wrongly, the parents believed this was the road to citizenship and a good life. In fact, the Beaupres might well have spent their entire life at Wabasha had not the issue of tribal enrollment raised its complicated head. Jim Beaupre's mother was Josette, a full-blood Ojibwe. Thus Jim was a member of the Pembina band from birth. He became separated from the band when he enlisted in the Minnesota Volunteers, went off to the War, and then settled in Wabasha. That same year the Pembina band sold its land to the government. By 1873 the government was pressed to create a home for the band, hence purchased a township on the western boundary of White Earth Reservation. When it came time to "enroll" these Ojibwe, Jim Beaupre was nowhere in sight. Thus his children were the only descendants of the Ojibwe Josette not to have been enrolled.

**Jim & Caroline Beaupre,
White Earth, 1907**

If there was ever a time for the Beaupres of Wabasha to relocate to the successor home of the Pembinas, it was in 1901. New policies were evolving, with a vocabulary to match—*allotment* and *apportionment*. For no other reason than the children, the Beaupres must move north to a place that even Jim had never visited—White Earth. And besides, he was not at all well, in fact, almost bedridden. At White Earth there would be an entire extended family, most of all Jim's older brother Joe and Joe's wife, the White Earth Medicine Woman!

Louise Beaupre: Newcomer at White Earth

Emily Peake's mother Louise (1886-1967),
daughter of Caroline and Jim Beaupre

> *Our first night on the reservation the Medicine Men were making Grand*
> *Medicine [Midewiwin] nearby. Suddenly from the swamp a great ball of*
> *fire was coming toward me. I was standing between the house and the fire*
> *ball. I had heard that if the ball stopped over the house, it was a bad omen.*
> *I focused my eyes on the fire ball and did not let it out of my gaze. Yes, it did*
> *recede. Then I knew I could find a good home at White Earth.*
> —Caroline Beaupre, undated

Just two of the Beaupre children made the journey with their
parents—oldest child Natalie (Nett) and youngest child Niles. It
was a difficult journey, with Father ailing and Nett assuming much
of the responsibility. Yet thirteen-year-old Niles considered the
train trip just one great adventure. A few personal belongings and
one or two pieces of furniture were all the family could manage to
take on the train. But not much would be needed since they would
be living with Uncle Joe and his wife, the White Earth Medicine
Woman, whom the children would remember as Aunt Mary.

Daughters Nell and Louise, ages twenty-two and fifteen,
followed some weeks later. Long afterward, Louise would record
the adventure for her own two daughters, Natalie and Emily, that
they might know a bit of the mystery that was White Earth:

> We bought our tickets in St. Paul. I didn't know anything about
> what to do. I was just following behind Nell, for she knew the
> way. The ticket seller looked at us from head to foot. He seemed
> quite bewildered. I remember the man saying, "Now, do you know

where you are going? It might be a little wild out there." But there was no need to tell Nell anything. She had taught at Billings right next to the Crow Agency. You couldn't scare her.

Louise's brothers Paul & Niles, Brother-in-Law Edwin Lerche, & nephew Billy Beaupre, "making wood" at White Earth, ca 1915

When we changed at Detroit for the train to Ogema, it was already loaded with Indians. Many were drunk and all were arguing and laughing. One of them wanted to pick a fight with the conductor because he wouldn't introduce them to us. I guess they were afraid of us. They all got off at Ogema and disappeared into the darkness. We also got off. It was pitch black. We finally saw someone with a lantern and asked if there were any wagons or carriages going to White Earth. "Ask that fellow over there," he told us. Sure enough it was Pete who drove the stage between the Ogema station and White Earth.

The stage was black with flap-like windows and four rows of seats, all facing the same direction. And there were the horses— those fiendish horses. A rather husky man was standing on the platform, which had one side higher than the other. The horses were pulled over to the high side while the man was holding their reins.

We climbed onto the stage and no sooner were seated than the horses reared up on their hind legs, pawing the air. I had my bird cage in one hand, with Molly Bird in it. In a flash I was jumping out on the platform, Molly Bird and all. . . . Finally Nell and I were able to get into the back seat, very gingerly with the little trunk, our suitcases and Molly Bird. Just ahead of us sat Mike LaChapelle, with Ben Fairbanks and some others. I don't remember their names. Finally Pete took his place. Once he had the reins, the horses were good and did what they were supposed to do.

Mike was the first to speak. He accused Pete of picking us up. Pete was silent. Then Mike began asking where we were going. Still Pete would not answer. Finally Mike guessed right. "They must belong to the old lady up there who dresses up so nice." Of course he meant Ma [Emily's Grandma Carrie], for she always had a sense of style. After that the others began to tease Mike and he left us alone.

Suddenly the stage stopped and Mike got out. The door of a little house opened and a woman in a funny hanging dress appeared. Her mouth was turned down in anger. She held a lamp high over her head. Her hair was drawn close to her head, tied in the back like a bermuda onion. She peered through the darkness to see who was getting off the stage. When she saw Mike coming to the door, she began cursing him in French. He hurried into the house. Bang went the door. Those on the stage just laughed.

At last we arrived at our destination. "This is it," said Pete, but we didn't get out. Nell and I thought it was the barn. Pete assured us, "No, this is the house and there is always somebody home. The old gentleman is there and they never leave him alone." Of course we knew he was talking about Pa. . . . Pete set our trunk and the suitcases on the ground, . . . bowed graciously and went on his way. . . . We went over to the house . . . and looked through a window. Yes, this was our house. We could see Pa's chair and our rugs from home. The door flew open and there was Ma.

We came into two big rooms. Off the living room was a bedroom, an alcove shut off by some curtains. That's where Pa was sleeping. A bright light burned in the kitchen, where a big table stood full of fresh bread and rolls. We didn't ask for any because we didn't know whose they were.

We learned that Uncle Joe had gone out with Aunt Mary, the Medicine Woman. She had gone to cure someone. Niles and Nett had gone along to watch how it was done. Now the door opened and in came Nett, dressed as if she were in the city. With her were [cousin] Edmund and Niles, also in their best clothes. The boys brought in our little trunk. Behind Nett and the boys was Aunt Mary, tall as a pine tree with dark hair very severely parted in the middle of her head and two long black braids down her back. She wore a blue checkered blouse that fit her perfectly. Yet in every buttonhole, where a button should have been, was a safety pin, as if it had been put there on purpose. She had on a full blue calico skirt and, needless to say, I was a little afraid of her. It was said that long ago when Uncle Joe was very sick, he had promised to marry her if she could save his life with her medicine. She did, and they were married right there in the Grand Medicine lodge.

Then in came Uncle Joe, who had had plenty of alcohol at the doctoring process. He came over and patted me on the head. Addressing Aunt Mary he said, "Our baby has come—this is our baby." Then both of them were kissing me and patting me on the head. I tried to wiggle away. I was afraid she might do something to me.

After that we all went to bed. Nell and I slept with Nett in one of the bedrooms upstairs. We were so scared we wouldn't have slept alone. That's when the trouble began. Soon Nell sat straight up in bed. "What's the matter with this bed? I feel like something is picking at me." And I sat up also. "Something is picking at me too." Then Nett told us. "You might as well know. There are fleas in this house." "Fleas!" cried Nell as she sprang out of bed. "I am not going to sleep in this bed any more." "That won't do any good. They are all around in the sand." So said Nett as she turned over and fell asleep. For some reason, they didn't bite her at all.

All night long we were pestered. I remember Nell ended up with a wash basin of soda water and a wash cloth, plus a hair brush for a scratcher. Just about that time we heard a voice outside singing, "Where's my wandering boy tonight." It was Uncle Joe, who had had far too much to drink. Somehow it all ended—the singing and the flea biting. In the morning things didn't seem so bad. The sun was shining. We came down to breakfast and found the table set with our own table cloth and our own dishes.

We all settled down at White Earth and Nell got a job on *The Tomahawk*.

Fred & Louise: The Newlyweds

The best way is to live in the present. Easy enough to preach but so hard to practice. We clutch the present nervously, with a backward glance at the past and one hand trying to ward off the future. The future with whatever it holds of good or ill is coming towards us relentlessly, inevitably. No amount of worrying or of pleasant anticipations will hurry or delay it.
—Louise Beaupre's Diary, 1910

The decade between Louise's 1901 arrival at White Earth and her 1911 marriage to Fred Peake was the worst of several bad decades in the history of the White Earth Reservation. Only a small fraction of the reservation land allotments were still in the hands of Ojibwe, the employment opportunities had vanished, and the great majority of the Ojibwe residents were destitute. Quite belatedly, the federal government had taken notice. Who was to blame? How was it that allotments belonging to full-blood Indians, to orphans, to other minors, even to the heirs of full-bloods, had all disappeared into corporate and private non-Indian hands? All this when federal law governing Indian land was intended to protect the special rights of full-bloods.

The first task was to define, then determine, who was a full-blood. The final determination would take up an entire decade, from 1910 to 1920. Investigation upon investigation was commissioned. The first investigation determined there was no such thing as a full-blood, given the long history of native and white encounters going back to the 16th century. Such a storm greeted this first determination that a "blood" census was taken in 1910. This time, 927 White Earth Indians were defined as full-bloods. This too was discredited. By 1913, federal attorneys had come to assume that a full-blood was a person with less than one-half "white blood." But this determination was promptly thrown out by the courts.

The final decision—the decision on which further litigation would be based—would not be handed down until 1920. The court would rule that precisely 512 of the original 5,173 White Earth allottees were full-bloods, of whom just 230 were still living. For these few, lawsuits against the corporate swindlers were now permitted to go ahead. What an opportunity this might have been for Fred Peake, the respected lawyer from Ogema—Fred Peake, whose sole interest had been to protect the land, the timber, and the people of his tribe. But for him the opportunity to stand up for the rights of his people came much too late. Fred Peake was a married man. No longer did he have the luxury of defending *pro bono* the rights of his tribe and his people. He was the family breadwinner.

For an educated mixed-blood at White Earth, the quickest, most lucrative path to financial security was real estate. Thus, in 1912, Fred Peake joined the lot of the successful mixed-bloods whom he had once despised. He began buying, brokering, and selling land on the White Earth Reservation.

The first two years of Fred and Louise's marriage found them living quite well in a fine home at Ogema. But like everything else in the world that was White Earth, the future was tentative at best. Any moment a capricious event might turn things upside down. More often than not, an omen, bad or good, would foretell the unexpected, if only one paid attention.

When news came in the summer of 1912 that Fred's brother George, newly married, would bring his bride Myrtle up to the reservation, Louise took notice. George had let it be known that Myrtle was the niece of Lord Russell in England. Preposterous, thought Louise. This must be an omen, but how indeed could one interpret it. Like Fred, George Peake had graduated from Carlisle Institute. During his student years, George had brought honor to Carlisle, in football, in baseball, and as a YMCA student leader. On the academic side, he won the school's gold medal for oratory. All in all, George Peake appeared to be a winner.

Thus the excitement at White Earth could hardly be contained. Out at Snyder Lake Isabel, mother of Fred and George, was cleaning house in a frenzy. Curtains were washed and pressed, bedding aired, and a guest room prepared for the royal daughter-in-law. Nor did Myrtle disappoint after she and George arrived. The newlyweds made the rounds of White Earth, George introducing his royal bride and Myrtle graciously accepting the oh's and ah's of the local citizenry. It was when they visited Ogema, home of Fred and Louise, that the real excitement began. Myrtle insisted on meeting Fred at his office. There she explained to him that she was about to receive $20,000 from her uncle, Lord Russell, in England, whose heir she was. She wanted to invest $10,000 of this money in land on the reservation, but she would like to do it right now. Fortunately, Fred knew of a large tract for which this amount would be perfect. In fact, it was land he hoped one day to acquire for himself. Myrtle proposed a plan that would benefit them all. Find ten men like Fred to invest $1,000 each. They and she would form a corporation so that they could purchase the land immediately. Then when her money arrived, she would put in $10,000, and each of the investors would get back his money. They'd all be shareholders together and it wouldn't cost the others anything. But why this generosity on Myrtle's part? Well, she believed in her husband George and she believed in his people. This was her way of being a part of White Earth.

The matter was urgent, since Myrtle and George would soon be on their way. Would Fred draw up the Articles of Incorporation immediately? Fred agreed. Also, he would gather other potential investors, and they would all meet in his office the following evening. And so they did, each one dressed his best in deference to the heiress. Fred brought along the paper he had prepared. Myrtle pulled out letters from Lord Russell and read them aloud—"To my dear niece Myrtle . . ." Yes indeed, $20,000 would be arriving shortly. The words were irrefutable.

Each man placed on the table his $1,000, an incredible sum at that time and place. But when it was Fred's turn, he demurred. "I want a little more time to consider. We shall not sign the Articles of

Incorporation tonight. Gentlemen, take back your money." George became so angry that he threatened to kill his brother. Fred coolly reached into his desk drawer and pulled out his gun. "Now we won't have any trouble here tonight." The men picked up their money and scattered, for they all knew well that Fred Peake was quite capable of using a gun.

After the others had left, Fred caught the night flier to St. Paul. He intended to look up Lord Russell's Minnesota property, as Myrtle had described it from the letters. He followed the directions exactly, expecting to find a wrought iron gateway with the name "Evansdale" written over the arch, and behind it a magnificent estate. He found nothing. Fred was outraged. On his return to Ogema, he demanded to see the Lord Russell letters. Clearly Myrtle had written them herself. Across the reservation, both Myrtle Peake, the heiress, and her husband George were now objects of derision. They promptly left town, and not surprisingly, their marriage disintegrated.[15]

But the entire episode almost unhinged poor Fred. He dared not face the once expectant investors after inviting them into an unusual opportunity, then later damning it all. Whether the others saw it in this way, we shall never know. But for Louise, whose White Earth roots were not so deep as her husband's, the disaster portended worse to come, an omen not to be ignored. Fred must move on, find a place where stability reigned, where he could practice the law as he understood it. Yet she dared not leave the reservation without the confirmation, long delayed, that she, as daughter of the deceased Jim Beaupre, was entitled to an allotment of White Earth land.

On the first of August 1913, the confirmation finally arrived. Nine months later, April 23, 1914, Baby Natalie was born. That summer Fred settled his affairs in Ogema, took his entire $1,000 in savings out of the bank, and with wife and child plus a trunk full of law books, boarded the train for Minneapolis.

American Girlhood

Minneapolis, City on the Move

In the first decade of the 20th century, Minneapolis was one of the fastest growing cities in the nation. It all began back in 1855, not long after the Dakota ceded virtually all their land in southern Minnesota to the United States. About that time a village sprang up on the east side of the Mississippi River, opposite the St. Anthony Falls. The French explorer, Father Louis Hennepin, had visited these falls back in 1680, naming them in honor of his patron saint. The new village also took the name St. Anthony. Just across the river, on the farthest reaches of the Fort Snelling military-reservation, a handful of white settlers and a scattering of Native Americans were already squatting along the bank in view of the falls and the village. By 1856 the government was forced to acknowledge their presence. Thus was born a second village, Minneapolis: Two villages, each harboring entrepreneurs intent on wresting profits from the surrounding forests, from the river, and above all, from the falls themselves.

In 1862 St. Anthony received a city charter; five years later Minneapolis also became a city. In 1872 the two cities were merged into one—Minneapolis, a city of 19,000, a river city, a sawmill center, and a railroad hub. A decade later the population had increased one and one half times to 47,000 while the railroads were reaching ever farther to the northwest and the sawmills multiplying exponentially. These were indeed extraordinary times.

By 1889 the river was jammed solid with logs from the lands upstream. The ongoing rape of the Ojibwe forests, coupled with the power harnessed from the Falls, had created an unprecedented prosperity that continued to fuel the city's phenomenal growth. But that was not all. The great prairie lands, once belonging to the Pembina, the Red Lake, the Mississippi, and later, the White Earth bands, now in the hands of others, were the source of a more permanent treasure—wheat, a hardy variety that grew exceedingly well in northern Minnesota. Now with a dense railroad network in place, immense flour mills were erected on the west side of the river at the Falls. Minneapolis had become the flour city of the nation, as well as the capital of the grain trade.

Expansion of the city landscape kept pace, as areas to the south, the north, and the west were rapidly incorporated. The piece east of the river, originally St. Anthony, soon merged with the western edge of St. Paul. Further south, the river itself would forever be Minneapolis's eastern boundary.

The city was not only growing, it was transforming itself. As early as 1905, what was left of Minneapolis's original site had so decayed that the city undertook the first of many urban renewal projects. By 1910 the lumber industry was finished, for the virgin timber forests were gone. But all of that barely slowed the city's growth. Minneapolis had become a Midwest hub in finance, banking, and commerce. Small manufacturing and a sizable clothing industry evolved, and whole residential areas came into being, driven by one of the most comprehensive street railway systems in the country. "Come, come, Minneapolis makes good!" So went the cry.

What high expectations must Fred Peake have had when he boarded the train for the city with Louise, Natalie, clothes, household goods, a typewriter, and his law books. In Minneapolis he would start over—set up his law office and from there work for justice and fairness, especially on behalf of his people. Best of all, he wouldn't be alone. Brother George, no longer burdened with the erstwhile heiress, was also in Minneapolis, alternately working as a laborer and a clerk, but studying evenings at Northwestern School of Law. Within two years George too should be admitted to the bar. So reasoned Fred. "Peake & Peake, Attorneys at Law": He could almost visualize their shingle outside an office on Nicollet Avenue.

But it wouldn't be that easy. What might an Indian lawyer expect in Minneapolis? By 1915 the population exceeded 333,000, with less than a hundred identifiable Indian residents. The power structure was solidly Yankee—men whose family names were all too familiar to Fred. He had fought and he had lost to lumber barons such as these. And the new immigrants? What could Fred do for them? Why, coming out of Scandinavia and Central Europe, they hardly spoke English! It wouldn't take long for Fred to figure this all out.

Family Matters I

Fred and Louise initially took a flat at No. 8 Grove Street. The flats were located on Nicollet Island, a wooded piece of land situated in the middle of the Mississippi River upstream from the Falls. The island contained some of the oldest homes in what was now Minneapolis, and the Grove Street Flats were arguably the most distinctive multi-residential building in the entire city. Built in 1877, they comprised six attached three-and-one-half-story residences topped by one giant mansard roof. Later architects would dub the style French Second Empire.* In 1915, however, Nicollet Island as a residential neighborhood had mostly been abandoned. Heavy manufacturing was rapidly settling in. It appears the Peakes stayed only briefly on the island. A year later they were living in cramped space at 515 East 28th Street. The law practice

---

* By the 1960s, the long dilapidated Grove Street Flats were scheduled for the wrecker's ball. Preservationists intervened and the Flats were saved. In 1983 they were restored, marketed, and sold as condominiums, a charming frontispiece to the newly renovated Nicollet Island neighborhood.

had been postponed but not forgotten, for the glass-front bookcase with Fred's law books occupied the most prominent space along the living room wall. For the time being, he was dealing in real estate. At this late date, one cannot be sure whether Fred was speculating himself or whether he was acting as broker for others. In a missive to the alumni office at Carlisle Institute, he wrote: "Not much of a money making man, but [I] get along well."

And little Natalie, now two years old? Often pensive, unusually sensitive to others' feelings, and most creative in her use of new words to express herself, she was indeed the delight of her father.

Natalie Peake, 6 years old
Minneapolis, 1920

In Natalie's small world, Father was all. Louise was the homemaker and indeed the stabilizing influence, for Fred's moods could range from unrealistic expectations to morose misgivings. Fortunately, Louise had been blessed with an optimistic world view and an even disposition—a calming element in the marriage when circumstances roused Fred's mercurial temperament.

From the Peakes' first day in the city, their residence was hotel, boardinghouse, and temporary home to relatives, and near-relatives from White Earth and wherever else the Beaupres and Peakes had settled. Even from the small apartment on East 28th Street, no one had ever been turned away. Louise would later laugh when recalling stepping over bodies in the early morning on her way to making coffee and fried bread. The joy of "family" overcame any inconvenience. Yet she longed for a more private home, a house with a porch and a garden, perhaps even a tree, such as she remembered from her Wabasha childhood. The opportunity came sooner than she might have expected. Fred did prosper briefly in the real estate market and by 1916 was able to purchase a rather new one-story house with an open front porch. It was located out on the periphery of the city. The address: 4413 - 29th Avenue South,* not far from Lake Nokomis, one of twenty-two lakes that were the pride and joy of the city.

In the spring of 1917 the United States entered the "war to end all wars," on the side of the Allies—World War I, as this horrendous conflict came to be known. The war had already dragged on for almost three years, engulfing most of Europe and causing massive casualties on both sides. The expectation was that it could last for years to come. The entire national economy quickly turned to the war effort, causing the real estate market to collapse and George Peake to abandon law school. George enlisted in the 78th Field Artillery, Sixth Division, and went off to Europe for seven months at the Front. The war marked the end of George's studies to become a lawyer. It also marked the end of Fred's real estate career and possibly the end of his hopes to practice law on Nicollet Avenue. As it turned out, the war ended much sooner than expected. With the United States providing a fresh input of men and machines, it was all over by November of 1918. United States casualties were relatively few. In fact, more American soldiers died in the 1918 flu epidemic than were killed in the hostilities.

That same year Fred hired on as "inspector" in the Washburn-Crosby flour mill down at St. Anthony Falls. Fred saw it as a temporary pause in his chosen career, the law. Yet for the first time in his life he had a regular paycheck. The decade that followed was by far the most stable period in Fred's life, the most secure economically, and probably the happiest years in his marriage. Yet even this idyllic time was not without its pain. Little Natalie, gentle Natalie, contracted spinal meningitis. She recovered but would

---

* In 1945 the one-time home of the Peakes and a number of other homes on 29th Avenue were torn down to make room for the post-WWII housing boom.

suffer a severe limp the rest of her life. This visible remnant of the dreaded disease never ceased to touch the deepest recesses of her father's heart.

In 1921 the Peakes left their suburban home on 29th Avenue and moved back into the central city. Why? Perhaps the proximity to the Washburn-Crosby mill, more likely Fred's dream of returning to the practice of law. When it came to Indian lands, the time was ripe. The final, final of the blood rolls had been ratified by the courts, giving birth to a new set of federal Indian policies. The Peakes were now living at 1606 - 5th Avenue South, which doubled as Fred's law office. Time to risk all by giving up his work at Washburn-Crosby. Fred was fearful that enrolled tribal members living off the reservations were in danger of being cut out of any potential largesse. Thus he sought out a few others from the tiny Twin Cities Indian community and organized The Twin Cities Chippewa Tribal Council. This Tribal Council forced the reservations and the federal government, for the first time, to acknowledge that an "Urban Indian" population was here to stay.[*]

We are told that Fred represented a number of clients out of his and Louise's extended families, which together encompassed much of the White Earth population. Yet eighty years later all that remain of his efforts are fragments of three files. These are no doubt representative, thus worth noting.

First, there was George Peake, who in 1922 applied to the White Earth Agency for his $100 annuity as legislated the previous November by the U.S. Congress. Before the war, George had borrowed $400 from tribal trust funds to finance his night law school. The White Earth Supervisor promptly denied payment of the annuity on the basis of this old loan. So outraged was brother Fred that he became the spokesman in a campaign to fund post-secondary education for enrolled members out of tribal funds. In the case of his brother George, Fred did succeed in securing the promised annuities, but it took a special Act of Congress.

---

[*] In the 1920s, Fred Peake's home cum law office was home not only to the Twin Cities Chippewa Tribal Council, but also to the Minneapolis Wigwam Welfare Society and the Twin Cities Indian Republican Club.

Then there was Louise, since 1910 enrolled in the Pembina tribe of her father, yet recognized only as an "adoptee" of the tribe. Even at this late date her application for back annuities deserves to be preserved, for it tells a great deal.

I claim my right to enrollment with the Pembina band of Minnesota Chippewas, on account of my grandmother Mrs. Josette Beaupre having been a full blood Indian woman of the Pembina Band. My father James Beaupre was the son of Josette Beaupre and was the only one of my grandmother's descendents that did not get enrolled under the Act of January 14th, 1889.

My father became separated from the Pembina Chippewa band by reason of serving in the Union Army during the Civil War. . . . My father always lived in Minnesota after returning from the war. . . . In later years my father removed to the White Earth reservation with his family. He lived and died there, and is buried there at the White Earth Agency in the Catholic cemetery. . . .

The Pembina people were never given an opportunity to declare their people for enrollment until 1911. Had my father been living in 1911 his people would have declared his enrollment. All of his children were recognized by the Pembina people at this first opportunity [1911] given them to enroll. Under the Treaty of 1889, the Pembina band . . . has full rights to the apportionments in the Minnesota Chippewa tribal fund. . . .

The descendants of my father James Beaupre that have any claim for back annuities are my brother Niles Beaupre who resides at White Earth, Minnesota, myself, and my niece Mary F. Bebout, daughter of my deceased sister. . . .

Louise Beaupre Peake, 4th day of April, 1924

Clearly the hand of Fred can be seen in his wife's petition. The claims of Louise and Niles were initially denied in 1927, but both Louise and Niles appealed. The affair would drag on until 1934, when poor Fred was no longer in a situation to be helpful. The claims for back annuities were totally rejected. The reasoning used was typical of the convoluted policies that continued to impoverish the land and the people. Hence key words are worth repeating in

65

this letter from the Commissioner of Indian Affairs dated June 1, 1934:

> *The records show that you were born away from the tribe [inWabasha], and did not affiliate therewith prior to 1905 or 1906; that you became a member of the tribe by adoption in 1910; that you have received tribal annuities paid subsequent to the date of your adoption; and that you are not entitled to payments made prior to that time. . . .To be entitled to tribal payment from date of birth, a person must be born into the tribe; that is, on the reservation among the Indians, and in affiliation therewith. As you were born away from the tribe, you were not born into the tribe, and did not become a member until your adoption which, as above stated, was not retroactive, but operated only to give you tribal rights from the date of the approval of the adoption by the Secretary of the Interior. . . .*

No mention was made that the father of the claimants had left the Pembina lands to serve three years in the Union Army, that afterward he had settled on non-reservation lands because at the time the Pembina Ojibwe were temporarily landless, that the family—hence claimants—had resettled on the reservation in 1901 when their father was ailing; or that Louise lived at White Earth until 1914 while Niles was still a resident of the reservation. Legal language ruled the day—language carefully designed to exclude.

In 1978 the Federal government reversed the 1934 Commissioner's opinion and determined that the Secretary of the Interior had no jurisdiction over the rights of a White Earth mixed-blood. Unfortunately, the rights of Louise Peake, Niles Beaupre and Mary Bebout, all deceased, had long been obliterated by decades of time.

Emily Louise Peake

(1920-1995), daughter of Louise and Fred Peake

May Day has past.
Mother's Day is here at last.
It brings joy to Father, Mother, Sister
Happy, Happy Mother's Day Greetings
from Abedieu
—Emily Peake, 1927

Emily was born on May 28, 1920, at Fairview Hospital in Minneapolis. She was named for her Aunt Emily as well as for her mother, Louise. The selection of names clearly indicated the parents' great expectations for this second daughter. Aunt Emily

Louise Peake with daughters Natalie & Emily
Minneapolis, 1924

Peake had already made a name for herself in a world far beyond Minnesota. After finishing Carlisle Institute, she had gone off to Washington and found employment with the Bureau of Indian Affairs. In fact, in 1910, when the allotment crisis at White Earth was at one of its many peaks, it was Emily Peake who was sent out to calm the waters and possibly fix those things that were fixable. Unfortunately, not much was fixable at that late date. Afterward Emily opened a women's clothing store in Washington—its name "The French Shop." And somewhere along the line she married a man from White Earth—Robitaille—who, before Oklahoma became a state, went out there to practice law. Emily Robitaille was a lifelong example as well as a loving aunt to Emily Louise.

Very early, Emily Louise became *Abedieu,* which later evolved into "Adieu." Whether "Abedieu" was simply the small child's mis-

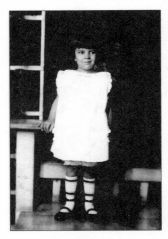

pronunciation of her own name, or her interpretation of some Chippewa word of endearment used by her father, has never been determined. One suspects the latter, for Fred Peake was fluent in the Ojibwe language, a legacy of early childhood. Just as Fred's grandmother Kah-goonce had once instilled in her daughter Keche-ogemah the language of their tribe and the lore of their dodem, so had Keche-ogemah—now Isabel Schneider—taught her oldest and most favored child the Chippewa language, instilling into him the power of their dodem, the crane.

Emily all dressed up, 1925

While Natalie, in spirit, resembled her father—the pensiveness, the sensibilities, the moods—little Emily very soon took on attributes of her mother. Once let loose in the neighborhood, she was inclined to bring home cats, dogs, and even neighboring children, any and all who she thought might benefit from her mother's hospitality. In this Mother never disappointed, even as economic difficulties multiplied. In 1926 Fred was forced to return to Washburn-Crosby, again as inspector. As a matter of fact, he was fortunate that his job was still available.

By that time, George Peake had found his own calling far removed from the law. Using the Soldiers Bonus given by the State of Minnesota to every World War I veteran, George had enrolled in drama and dance at Minneapolis's MacPhail School of Music. His muse: the great interpretive dancer Ted Shawn.* In 1921 George graduated from MacPhail and before long evolved into *Little Moose, the Chippewa Chief*. For many years, he and his troupe of dancers

Stand Rock Indian Ceremonials, The Dells, WI, 1930
Emily, front row, second from left

performed the "Stand Rock Indian Ceremonials" at the Dells resort area in Wisconsin. Even young Emily spent several summers at the Dells, living with Uncle George and his second wife, Aunt Maude. Dressed in an exotic Indian ceremonial dress cleverly crafted by her mother, Emily more than held her own with the adult dancers. Uncle George later insisted that little Emily, not Chief Little Moose, was the real star.

---

* Ted Shawn (1891-1972) reached international fame by remaking the public view of male dancers. Shawn created a dance technique built upon essentially masculine actions. Some of his greatest dance solos were based on American Indian themes.

Depression/Depression

One cannot say for sure which came first—Fred Peake's gradual decline into mental illness or the nation's rapid decline into the Great Depression.

For Fred, one might say that the onset was in 1928. Washburn-Crosby Mills became General Mills through a consolidation that involved a number of western and Midwestern milling companies. The celebrated merger cost Fred Peake his job. He was forced to become a day laborer. For the next three summers, he was digging ditches by hand, helping to lay pipes in the city streets as the public sewer system grew and grew, barely keeping pace with the expanding city residential areas. During the cold Minnesota winters he signed in daily at the "day labor" office, sometimes succeeding in getting a few hours' work, more often not.

In 1929 Fred's mother, Isabel Peake Schneider—once upon a time Keche-ogemah—died at White Earth. This was the woman who taught him so much of what he knew and who believed in him above all. Her death devastated this son, especially since he had been in no position to care for her during her last illness.

Then, in October of that year, the New York stock exchange "crashed," throwing the nation's financial world into a tailspin. At first the economic impact was not felt directly in Minnesota, but by the winter of 1931-32, the full severity of the disaster had engulfed the entire state. Even in Minneapolis the "day labor" jobs dried up. Fred Peake no longer was able to earn money. He became increasingly agitated over the general state of affairs, especially his inability to support a family. He found it ever more difficult to control his temper, and following each such outburst, would sink into moroseness.

Louise attempted to smooth every situation, always expressing hope that it would all soon turn around. Fred's law books were still the defining feature of their small living room. It was Emily's duty to dust the bookcase daily and from time to time wash the glass doors. Louise believed and Louise insisted: Frederick Peake, Jr., was still a lawyer, and one day he would practice again.

Fortunately, Fred could always count on the quarterly checks from the Mississippi Band Trust. These funds were under direct control of the federal government, whose management the Ojibwe never quite trusted. Some quarters nothing arrived. Other times $10, sometimes as much as $23, and occasionally a "capital" share of $100, which at that time was a goodly sum. Yet these bits and pieces were paying the rent. When it came to food, Louise had no fear of the "breadline," which often netted much more than a loaf of bread. One day Louise received a beef pot roast, which called for a celebration. She invited over two of Emily's girl friends so as to make it a true festivity. The family also benefited from the city's miniscule "general relief," and once in a while Louise succeeded in doing housework for a family slightly better off than her own. When Fred discovered that his wife had "hired out," he exploded in anger, then fell still deeper into depression.

Always Natalie and Emily were on Louise's mind. Time to move to a more residential area, perhaps a duplex flat. And so it came about. That spring the Peakes moved their modest belongings, along with Fred's typewriter, his files, the law books, and the bookcase, to a duplex at 2537 5th Avenue South. Their second-floor flat, including an additional bedroom, was larger than the apartment. The neighborhood was to some extent mixed—mostly white, a few Blacks, and a smattering of Indians. It must have been a very small smattering, for according to the 1930 census there were but 158 identifiable Indians in the city out of a population of 464,356 inhabitants. Whatever the mix, this was a family neighborhood, a middle-class neighborhood where most every family was at least temporarily poor; 2537 would be home to the Peakes for the next thirty years.

Oddly enough, at White Earth, once the most destitute place in the state, good things were happening. Franklin Roosevelt became president in January of 1933, promising a "New Deal for the American people." He brought with him a Congress ready to do whatever it took. By spring, the administration had already announced job programs with acronyms that would live far beyond the programs themselves—CCC, NYA, and WPA.* All of these were promised for the White Earth Reservation, as well for the entire nation. High hopes for those who had almost lost hope.

Fred and Louise Peake in Minneapolis, 1930

That winter it became very clear to Louise, probably to Fred also, that he simply could not go back to the Minneapolis sewer department. He was now close to age sixty-two and weakened physically as well as mentally. But Fred had not quite yet given up. He fretted out loud that unless he could pull himself together,

---

* Civilian Conservation Corp, National Youth Administration, Work Projects Administration

the little family simply would not survive in the city, even if a satisfactory job became available. If worse came to worse, might they not return to White Earth? Others before them had done that, and there was certainly no shame in it. Always there were visitors coming by, family and friends from White Earth. They might stay a night or two on their way to Washington to plead for the band. They might stay longer, weeks even, in the hope of finding work and not finding any. Louise never complained, for hospitality was in her blood. No matter how scarce the money, she would put on the table a breakfast of coffee, bacon, and fried bread, Ojibwe style, enough for any and all who came by.

Always visitors brought gossip from the reservation, much of it having to do with land. Fred, who years before had sold his own land allotment, now entertained the thought of acquiring enough land at White Earth, to pitch a tipi and plant a garden at the minimum, eventually to build a house. Never mind that neither Fred nor Louise had ever lived in a tipi. The best that could be said was that Fred's mother was born in a wigwam* along the Mississippi River and Louise's father had spent a childhood of summers in tipis on the Minnesota prairie. To Fred, in his better moments, all things were possible. And even if things didn't work out, there would always be the land.

When it came to his attention that St. Michael's parish in rural Mahnomen County had moved the church to the town of Mahnomen and was offering its church site—forty acres—for sale, Fred seized the moment. Unbeknownst to Louise, he wrote on her behalf to the Chippewa Agency at Cass Lake and placed an offer for the land, including a small earnest money order. This time the superintendent was on their side. He replied immediately, explaining that back in 1908 the site had been awarded to the Catholic Independent Missions as a church site and later signed over to St. Michael's. But since the St. Michael parish had moved off the land, the tract by law reverted to the United States government. And what a tract it

---

*Unlike the tipi, a cone-shaped buffalo hide structure widely used by Plains tribes, the wigwam is a dome-shaped dwelling made of bent saplings covered with grass mats or bark, typical of the Woodland tribes.

was—not forty, but eighty acres—open land plus cutover forest with a modicum of new growth. The superintendent further stated that Louise Beaupre, an adopted member of the Pembina band, had never taken her land allotment. It was almost too good to be true. Fred wrote out the application by hand, for he was no longer able to manage a typewriter.

On May 30, on his sixty-second birthday, Fred Peake made a serious attempt to kill himself. He did not succeed. The authorities intervened, and Fred was promptly hospitalized, declared incompetent, and sent to the Minnesota State Hospital at Rochester. The grim diagnosis: "manic depressive psychosis, manic type."

Louise would eventually receive her allotment. She intended to keep the land as security for her daughters' futures. But the Depression seemed to have no end; one after the other, she sold the two pieces, that the family might hold out a bit longer. And the quarterly payments from the Mississippi Band Trust? Whatever was yet to be paid out in Fred's name now belonged to his new caregiver, the State of Minnesota.

Natalie Peake

Emily's older sister (1914-1990), daughter of Louise and Fred

Natalie was a beautiful, intelligent young woman,
something of a writer: sensitive, an easily broken reed.
—Childhood friend Frances Green Anderson

In most ways, Louise was much like her own mother Caroline Beaupre, who died in 1926. She was eighty-two years old and had outlived eight of her ten children. At White Earth, Grandma Carrie's name was still spoken of with awe—the tiny lady who nevertheless stood tall, who spoke with a "French" accent (though it was probably more Mississippian than French), who was darker in color than most of the White Earth Indians, who even in near poverty dressed "like Paris," and who loved every child she ever met. Caroline had her own special name for her favored daughter Louise—*Mon Amie*. Over the years, *Mon Amie* became "Amie," the name by which Louise would be known throughout her life, among friends as well as within the family. Like her mother, Louise was not to be bent, neither psychologically nor physically. It is said that she never forgave Fred for abandoning her and the children by trying to kill himself. Yet, she taught her daughters to take pride in their father. He was the orator—the crane—who always had worked for justice, especially for the Indian people. The bookcase with Fred's law books continued to stand solemnly in the living room, a reminder of who Papa had once been and who he might once again be.

The problem, which later became the second great family tragedy, was Natalie—Natalie, the poet, the writer, gentle Natalie, beautiful Natalie, who nearly collapsed after her father's failed suicide, and who after that was never the same. At the time, Natalie was a freshman at the University of Minnesota, but she soon dropped out and began to roam the streets. Like so many others, Natalie was unemployed. She was still living at home, but hardly there. She was a terrible worry to her mother, Amie, for this daughter was now involved in a political movement that Louise simply could not understand.

Which brings us to one of the defining episodes in the history of Minneapolis—the 1934 Truckers' Strike. This strike remains an epic event in American labor history. The strikers were members of a fledgling organization of truck drivers, Local 574 of the Teamsters Union. Their intent: To win recognition as a union and to bargain collectively within the city of Minneapolis. It was a bitter struggle, this strike that lasted some six months. And it would change forever the economic life of a city that had formerly prided itself on being "non-union."[*]

---

[*] The 1934 Truckers' Strike was fraught with violence. The historic May 22 confrontation at Market Square resulted in massive injuries, including two deaths, one of which is well-covered in the essay "Death in Market Square," by the author (see Bibliography.)

Members of Local 574 were men—truck drivers—but the women were behind them and a force to be reckoned with. Every day and all night, they ran the strikers' kitchen—coffee with buttermilk, vats and vats of thick stew, and bread, always bread. Wives, girlfriends, factory workers idled by the truckers' picket lines, students from the university, the unemployed—yes, even Natalie Peake—were out in force. For the first time in her life, this young Indian woman with a definite limp was accepted for what she had to give, and even more important, for what she had come to believe in.

Enter the charismatic Meridel LeSueur,* a Minnesota writer and literary critic of some renown, a popular lecturer in the best Minneapolis circles, a political radical, and part Indian though it was never clear as to what part. Meridel covered the Truckers' Strike as a reporter, taking special note of this cadre of women. It is not known whether or not she actually helped serve meals. But afterwards she wrote a riveting short story, "I Was Marching,"† which describes this piece of the drama that no historian has bothered to document. Natalie too was there. Thus did she meet the woman who would become her inspiration and her mentor.

The Truckers' Strike finally ended, but only after Governor Floyd B. Olson called a meeting of the employers at the Capitol. He is said to have strode into the room and challenged them with words to the effect, "You are going to have to settle eventually. I advise you to do it now." They did, and the strike was over. Overnight Minneapolis had become a unionized city, with the Teamsters Union representing much more than just the truckers.

---

* Even before her death in 1996, Meridel LeSueur had become a legend, especially in feminist circles. Recognized in the 1930s for her talents and her causes, eclipsed in the fifties and the sixties for her Communist connections, and re-emerging in the eighties as a significant writer of feminist/socialist fiction and non-fiction, Le Sueur's life and works continue to be celebrated.

† Originally published in the *New Masses,* a left-wing periodical not affiliated with the American Communist party. In 1940 the story was republished as part of a LeSueur collection entitled *Salute to Spring* (see Bibliography.)

The following January, between lectures and her own writing, Meridel LeSueur opened a weekly evening writing class downtown. From the first meeting on, Natalie was there. She too would be a writer, documenting the plight of the laboring classes. She need only think of dear Papa—the ditch digger, the day laborer—and know that he too had been there.

March 14, 1935, four days after Louise Peake's forty-ninth birthday: That morning the sun was shining with spring in the air, even though snow still lay on the ground. Besides, the times could have been worse. Natalie finally had found a clerical job of sorts. Evenings she was busy at home writing, once a week reading aloud in Meridel LeSueur's classroom. Emily was in her last year of junior high school, earning satisfactory grades and doing her bit at home, as if housework were play, all in all joining her mother in keeping the little Peake household a happy place. Always there was the hope that one day Papa would return and it would all be as it had once been.

That morning down at the Rochester State Hospital for the Insane—so it was called—the sun was also shining with spring in the air, even though snow still lay on the ground. But in the infirmary ward, the patient Fred Peake lay desperately ill with bronchopneumonia. It had been diagnosed ten days earlier and had only gotten worse. His body was being consumed by a raging fever. A nurse stood nearby. Quite suddenly the patient raised himself from his near-coma and looked toward the window. "Nurse, my dodem called to me just now."

Then he lay back and died. It was 10:30 in the morning.

School Days

Emily always said she was French and English, and that her father was a
lawyer. But we all knew she was an Indian and that her father had tried
to kill himself.
—Childhood friend Lorraine Dixon (Dixie) Campbell

Fred Peake's funeral was held in Minneapolis, with an Episcopal
priest presiding, for that was his church, and since her marriage
Louise's also. Fred was buried at Acacia Cemetery in St. Paul.
Louise saw to it that, at least for a moment, what most defined her
husband beyond family would be remembered. His obituary in the
Minneapolis Tribune read in part:

> *Mr. Peake was born at Crow Wing, Minn., and received his early education*
> *at Carlisle, Pa. He later attended Dickinson College in Philadelphia, and*
> *the North Dakota College of Law at Grand Forks, N.D. Mr. Peake was*
> *a member of the firm of Fargo and Peake, the first law firm established*
> *in Ogema, Minn., and was the first mayor of the town when it was*
> *incorporated in 1907. Mr. Peake was active in affairs of the Chippewa*
> *Indian tribe, and 12 years ago was instrumental in obtaining national*
> *legislation for the education of Chippewa youths. He was a member of*
> *Park Lake Lodge No.254, A.F. & A.M. Mr. Peake is survived by his wife; two*
> *daughters, Natalie and Emily; two sisters . . . and two brothers . . .*

As was the custom in the Park Lake Lodge, Fred's lodge brothers
paid for a suitable marker at his grave site.

Life must go on, and America would make it through these hard
times. So had the president promised, and so did Louise believe.
Natalie and Emily were the future, and that's where she, their
Amie, would be. Emily had many friends in the neighborhood, and
she invariably invited them home to the family flat. Amie could

be counted on to find a homemade cookie and, if not a cookie, at least a piece of leftover fried bread with marmalade. Emily liked showing off Amie, for Amie could brighten anyone's day. Emily also had a best friend Midge,* who lived across the street. Midge's father too had been a lawyer, and he too had died. (At 15, Emily was too embarrassed to admit that her father had only recently died, in a hospital for the insane.) But Midge wasn't the only best friend. There was Frances,† whom Emily had met when they were in confirmation class together at Gethsemane Episcopal Church. Gethsemane was a downtown church, the oldest Episcopal church in the city. Its membership was a curious mixture—a few of the old and "best" families who no longer lived in the neighborhood and several Indian families, whose roots went back to Father En-megah-bowh and Bishop Whipple. Emily and Frances were confirmed together.

Since they attended different schools, Saturdays were their time together, with a sleepover to Sunday, then down to Gethsemane with their mothers. Sleepovers at Emily's were always an adventure. Likely as not, there would be one or two temporary guests from White Earth, and always there would be at least one refugee animal that Amie had adopted. In the spring of 1934, the rescued animal was a large white rabbit, trained to a sandbox on the back stairway. Amie insisted that the rabbit's presence not be broadcast about. But one Saturday afternoon, with Frances sleeping over, the girls let the rabbit run about in Emily's room.

The doorbell rang from below. Father Urquehart, the Indian priest, had come to make a formal parish call. Amie was her hospitable self, taking his hat and coat, inviting him to sit down near the oil stove, rustling up tea and cookies, then joining him for a discussion of whatever mattered at the moment. Emily and Frances could not contain their curiosity. From Emily's room they opened the door a little bit to watch the tea party. In a flash, the white rabbit hopped out and across the living room. They dared not

---

* Margaret Ann Kranz, whose memories have helped flesh out these chapters.
†Frances Lee Green Anderson, whose own memoirs have contributed substantially to these chapters

come out to catch it. Yet the rabbit could have been invisible for all the attention it attracted. Amie blanched at the sound of the door but refused to cast her eyes on the rabbit. And the priest? He was giving his most rapt attention to whatever she had to say. When it was time to leave, Amie handed Father Urquehart his hat and coat; he took her hand and, with a formal blessing, left the flat. The girls were dumbfounded. Had the grownups really not seen the rabbit? Only then did Amie confront the girls. "Well?" That was all she said, but they knew. Years later, Frances would say it was the only time she had ever seen Emily's mother angry and she didn't even raise her voice.

There were other Saturday adventures in the Fifth Avenue flat. Once a month the Indian Women's Club, the Sah-Kah-Tay Club, usually seven or eight women, met in Louise's living room. Frances remembers how poor the women seemed and how strangely dressed, especially their shoes. Louise was always in charge, with tea and sandwiches, encouraging a friendly bantering that was mixed with much laughter. Afterward she would tell the girls about living on the reservation, the good times and the poverty, and how these Indian mothers were struggling to find a place in the life of a strange city.

At Phillips Junior High School, Emily picked up two more best friends, Dixie and Iney.* Dixie lived on Portland Avenue just across the alley from Emily. Both girls loved movies, and when they could tease a nickel out of their mothers, they would walk downtown to the theater, especially when Shirley Temple was playing. So captured were they by Shirley's tap dancing, especially with Bojangles, they could sit through the film twice and would have added a third round had not the mothers forbade it. The mothers considered movie theaters poor places for their daughters. For a nickel a homeless man could sleep in the darkened theater from noon until midnight, and more than a few did.

Emily and Dixie wanted more than anything in the world to dance. They actually found a teacher of tap dance, and somehow put

---

* Lorraine Dixon Campbell and Inez Nelson Sandness.

together enough money for a single lesson. There was never enough money for a second lesson, but that didn't matter. All winter and all summer they practiced. They practiced every night and in summer much of the day. Both of the girls became very good, especially Emily, and they never quit, not even in high school. Every year they performed at school assemblies and Emily, in her senior year, tap danced her way to first prize in the talent show.

In those junior high summers Emily and Dixie wrote plays, always with just two characters. The little dramas were about college sorority girls. The young playwrights didn't really know what a sorority was, but that didn't stop them. They set up a stage in the attic of Emily's duplex and invited the younger children from the neighborhood. At first the children wouldn't come because of the attic heat. Emily solved that problem. She bought a bag of penny candy. Each child who attended a performance was rewarded with a piece of candy. Now the children always came no matter what the temperature.

Emily loved to read, but there was no public library in the neighborhood. When it was allowed at school, she would carry home a book to devour overnight—especially fairytales from anywhere. She knew the Grimm Brothers' and Anderson's fairytales almost by heart. Whenever there was a new edition of either collection, Emily would bring it home, read the familiar tales once more, and hope a new tale might have turned up. Emily dreamt of kings and queens; she dreamt of being French; she dreamt of being English. In those years she probably never dreamt of being an Indian, for it was all too real in her life.

Bit by bit, Emily was pushing out from the neighborhood. A favorite destination was the Minneapolis Institute of Arts, a great white-pillared edifice just three blocks from home. This became Emily's escape from whatever she found humdrum in the real world. Often on a Saturday, with Dixie in tow, Emily would visit her favorite Institute haunts, beginning with the tall stone fountain from the Italian Renaissance surrounded by live ferns, water dripping from the top of three concentric pools. The fountain stood in an interior patio just beyond the entrance hall. Such a lovely sound the water made. Always Emily brought with her a penny, to make a wish and throw it into the lowest pool. From there, her chosen path led directly to the Institute Period Rooms. These were elaborate reconstructions of European and American rooms, each enclosed by the original paneled walls and windows retrieved from some great residence and furnished with items of the time—from England, from France, and from colonial America. At the doorway to each room, Emily and Dixie would lean against the rope, their heads as far into the space as possible, then imagine themselves at a tea table, in a game of cards, or being courted on the love seat, all in all transported to a place and time far removed from here and now.

Certainly they must also have toured the painting collections on the second floor, but Emily was never comfortable ascending the great marble staircase. At the top of the stairs hung the most famous treasure at the Institute, Rembrandt's painting of "Lucretia." Beginning at the bottom of the stairs, all the way up, one could not help but watch Lucretia with her infinitely sad countenance, one hand on the bloody dagger pulled from her breast, the other clutching the bell cord to summon her maid. Always Lucretia's suicide reminded Emily of Papa's demise, the infinite sadness that near the end too often shone on his face.

The Belladettes

Emily had such a wonderful sparkle that said 'come along.' Her lifelong playfulness masked the darker side of her personal and family experiences.
—Lifetime friend Frances Green Anderson

In the fall of 1935, best friends Emily, Midge, Dixie, and Iney entered Central High. The school, like the neighborhood, was mixed—mostly Whites, also some Blacks. The Indian students, if any, were invisible. But the students all had something in common. Their families were poor, often very poor, and no one really took notice.

At Central High, the four girls from Phillips picked up Clarice and Vivian Roisen. They all became inseparable. Of the six, Emily was the best student, the originator of grand plans, the mother hen, so to speak. Central High was full of clubs, especially girls' clubs. If you were in one, you were *in*. If not, you weren't. Not one of the six was in a club. Said Emily, "We shall have our own." Thus was born the Belladettes. They met once a week in each other's homes and did whatever they thought club girls were supposed to do. Mainly they supported each other. If there was a dance and one of the girls had no date, the others arranged a blind date. Emily was a superb dancer and she loved to dance. Yet most often it was she for whom the others found a partner. Eventually she gave up on the high school dances. As it turned out, Emily never had an ordinary date in high school. Nobody talked about it, but the Belladettes knew. Emily was an Indian.

George Peake (Chief Little Moose), undated

Emily had a dream, and it had all started when she danced in the "Indian Ceremonials" with Uncle George—Chief Little Moose. George was still performing summers at the Wisconsin Dells, but otherwise he lived in New York. In the late 1930s, Chief Little Moose was the rage, New York's authority on Indian "music, dances, songs and legends taken directly from the woodlands, deserts and plains of North America." So said the city's *Metropolitan Host*. With Aunt Maude at his side, George was weathering the Depression quite well. She, a nurse, always had work. And when Chief Little Moose performed at the likes of Rockefeller Center's glamorous Rainbow Room, he brought home fees that more than matched Maude's.

In 1938 Emily's ambitions did not include Indian dance. She wanted to be a "modern" ballet dancer. How many times had Uncle George told her about the genius of Ted Shawn and his wife Ruth St. Denis, who was at least as famous? Emily knew about Minneapolis's MacPhail School of Music and Dance, where Uncle George had once studied. Even in high school, Frances was already taking voice lessons with a well-known MacPhail teacher. The MacPhail dance teacher, Lillian Vail, had actually studied with Ted Shawn. Emily's dream was to attend the MacPhail School, study modern dance under Miss Vail, and become a famous dancer. In the late 1930s, there was no way for her even to begin. It was difficult for Emily to give up the dream, but finally she did.

In the spring of their senior year, the Belladettes decided to join Minneapolis Society. How did one enter Society? The girls didn't really know, but they regularly read the Society section of the *Minneapolis Tribune* and decided to explore the possibility. They manufactured an announcement, which Emily typed out and submitted to the *Tribune*.

"The Belladettes of Central High School will honor their mothers with a combined Mother's Day dinner for all the Belladette mothers. Hostesses for the event are Lorraine Dixon, Margaret Ann Kranz, Inez Nelson, Emily Louise Peake, Clarice and Vivian Roisen."

To their delight, the *Tribune* published the announcement on the Society page. But soon the delight turned to guilt. The girls never did invite their mothers to a Mother's Day event, let alone a dinner.

What separated the Belladettes from the other clubs at Central was its longevity. Soon after graduation, Clarice and Vivian moved out of the state. Except for the years when Emily too was away, the four remaining Belladettes met once a month, up until the month Emily died. Even in the year 2003, with Midge and Iney in a nursing home, once a month Dixie's daughter drives her mother to the care center so that the three Belladettes can reminisce about Emily and the times of their youth.

Emily and Midge and Dixie and Iney and Clarice and Vivian all graduated from high school in June of 1938. Emily had taken the high school commercial course—typing, shorthand, accounting— and she had done very well, a "whiz," according to Frances, who was a half-year behind them. Emily had also taken two years of French

**Emily Peake, Central High School
graduate, Minneapolis, 1938**

and did extraordinarily well. She was making grand plans for her life. Someday she would go to college, and one day she would travel to Europe. Right now, though, Emily had to find a job. Her mother depended on it, and Baby Jacqueline depended on it. Yes, there was now a new member of the family. Two months earlier, Natalie had given birth to a little girl with a perfectly round face and a head full of jet black hair, the most beautiful baby Emily had ever seen. But Natalie promptly turned the infant over to Amie, saying, "I have no idea how to be a mother."

Breaking Away

A World Not So Kind

Where are you from? You don't look to be from here.
　　　　　　—Federal Reserve Bank job interviewer,
　　　　　　　　　looking Emily over, 1938

It was really quite surprising. In 1938 a bit of the nation's economy had picked up, but the unemployment rate was still totally unacceptable. Minneapolis was actually one of the brighter spots, and five of the six Belladettes immediately found jobs. Only Emily, the one most in need of a paycheck, had no job. Emily, the star of the commercial course, with better grades than the other five Belladettes, was interviewed and interviewed but never hired. When the personnel woman at the Federal Reserve Bank doubted Emily's authenticity, Emily was close to exploding, but she did not. She only reiterated pleasantly that she was born in Minneapolis and afterward blurted out to friend Frances all that had taken place. Later Frances would recall the devastating impact this seemingly innocuous query had had on her friend. It was a blow Emily would not forget.[16]

With two daughters now unemployed and Baby Jackie to be cared for, with house cleaning opportunities few and far between, Louise was forced to visit the Minneapolis Welfare Department. Carrying the infant in her arms, she stated her predicament to the welfare worker. Was there any way of getting help from the family of the child's father? He had offered to marry Natalie, the baby's mother, provided she would go to Alaska with him. Natalie had refused, and he went alone. The young man's father? He had a good job and was on the Minneapolis School Board. The social worker almost laughed in Louise's face: "Forget it. Why, he is big in the Farmer-Labor Party and you're just an Indian."

Natalie was immersed in her writing. She now was part of the Writer's Workshop, a WPA program where published writers could

WPA worker Emily Peake;
Minneapolis Public Library 1940;
John P. Rossiter family collection,
MHS

teach and mentor the would-be's. At home she wrote and she wrote. Meridel LeSueur had taken a very personal interest in Natalie, recognizing both talent and fragility in this eager young woman. When it became imperative that Natalie now had a little daughter to support, Meridel even helped arrange a position for her—as librarian at the Minneapolis Labor School. This too was a WPA program, and it meant a paycheck, small as it was.

The WPA: Yes, Emily had hoped to do better. She was very attractive, a little pixie, one might say, with her straight black hair now set each night in pin curls to match the style of the times, always looking fresh in her one and only pair of silk stockings, black pumps, black purse to match, a simple skirt and blouse, never without her bright smile and outgoing ways—yet Emily couldn't find a job. There was no other choice. Emily too signed on with the WPA. At least the placement woman recognized some unusual potential. Emily was sent to work at the Minneapolis Public Library.

Her first week at the library, Emily phoned Frances, who was also now employed downtown. "Come over to the library; we'll have lunch in the cafeteria." When Frances arrived, Emily met her on the stairway. She had just learned about the library lunch rule and she didn't like it at all. In the employees' cafeteria, the WPA workers were required to eat together at a table quite separate from the others. Emily refused. Instead the two friends sat outside on the library steps, eating their bag lunches and commiserating with one another. Emily may have felt a bit demeaned, but at least both she and Natalie had paychecks to support the little family at home— Amie and Jackie, now an adorable four-year-old. Years later, Jackie would write:

> *Amie, my grandmother, was always putting up friends and relatives. She was very, very social as was Emily with her friends. I remember Mr. Jorgensen, who spent a lot of time resting and talking at our house, and Mr. Tomahawk, who stayed for two years. People from the reservation would often come down. I can still hear the warm, humming sounds of activity that surrounded me. I was pretty special, too.*

In December of 1941, everything changed, and it all happened so suddenly. On Sunday, the seventh, Japanese planes bombed Pearl Harbor in Honolulu, where much of the United States Pacific fleet was docked. Most of the battleships were sunk; many, many sailors killed. The following day, President Roosevelt asked the U.S. Congress for a declaration of war. The Congress voted to declare war, with but one nay vote. Congress could hardly do otherwise, for Japanese forces were already invading the Philippine Islands, an American outpost in the Pacific.

But that wasn't all. A great European war was already in progress. In the fall of 1939, Germany, under Adolf Hitler and the Nazis, had invaded Poland, and by December of 1941 Germany controlled most of the European continent, including vast areas of the Soviet Union. Germany and Japan had a mutual defense treaty that obligated Germany to declare war on any Japanese belligerent. Thus the United States' declaration of war on Japan triggered the German declaration of war on the United States. Subsequently, on December 11, the United States Congress declared war on Germany.

In fact, the United States was already helping the beleaguered British Isles by sending material aid to England, although Roosevelt was roundly criticized for these efforts. But now, at the end of 1941, there was a sea change in the nation. Every activity, economic and otherwise, would have to play a part in arming the nation for what amounted to two separate wars, each against a most powerful enemy. Suddenly young men were enlisting in droves. And those who didn't enlist would soon be drafted, for a selective service system had already been put in place.

The WPA program tasks were promptly altered, all to serve the war effort. In another year, these programs would all but disappear. Eventually, Natalie and Emily would find better jobs, each in a "war plant," as most manufacturing industries came to be known. For Emily, this meant making parachutes at the Honeywell plant near her home. Now she was in a position to take a few courses at the University. Almost every evening she rode the streetcar to the university campus, studying on the way, both forth and back.

Even Amie—Louise—found her niche in the war effort, although she didn't quite view it that way. The young Ojibwe men, no different from their black and white brothers, were going off to fight the war. The WPA reservation programs were fading fast, and scores of young Ojibwe women from northern Minnesota, many of them hardly more than teenagers, were arriving in the city, finding jobs. For them Amie feared the most. She was still close to the tribulations of Natalie's adolescent years, and she would wish all that on no one. Thus Amie let it be known that the Na-gu-aub Club was meeting in her home. Word spread fast in the community—in 1942 there were fewer than two hundred Indian residents in the entire city—and the club was born. Each Saturday ten or more young women met at Amie's home. There they could put their frustrations, their fears, their ambitions into words. Amie listened well. Frequently, there was laughter, sometimes even tears, and always tea and homemade cookies. The Na-gu-aub Club was thriving, a comfortable refuge in a strange city.

The Na-gu-aub (Rainbow) Club, Louise Peake standing on the right, undated. Club members: Mary Bagley, Josephine Cloud, Delia Defoe, Josephine Defoe, Marion English, Catherine Godfrey, Maxine Hodder, Elsie Johnson, Bessie Lawrence, Frances Littlewolf, Lily Parkhurst, Louise Pine, Clytha Rose, Philomine St. Clair, Jessie Smith, Bernice Swan, Dora Thomas, Helen Trotterchaud, Bernice Vanoss. Not all are pictured.

Such a Wasted Life

Amie's flat provided temporary lodging for almost anyone from the northern Ojibwe lands. The back bedroom had sleeping space for one, two, three, or more guests. Some nights even the living room was turned into a sleeping room. Emily now had the tiny room off the living room while Amie and Jackie (and Natalie when she was at home) shared the front bedroom. But Natalie was mostly somewhere else. She had quite suddenly married one Glen Blanch, whom she knew from the Minneapolis Labor School. This was a good turning point in Natalie's life, for Glen seemed to be a stable, sober young man, and he adored little Jackie. So reasoned Amie and Emily, for they had often discussed the dangers that threatened Natalie. She was known to drink beer. Besides, her radical political friends could easily bring danger not only to Natalie, but to all of them.

Late in 1942, Glen Blanch went off to war, eventually to fight the Japanese in the Pacific theater. For Natalie, Glen's departure was almost as devastating as her father's hospitalization. Still, in

**Jackie and Adieu
Minneapolis, 1941.**

February of 1943 she obtained work at the Twin Cities Ordnance Plant in New Brighton, just north of the city. This should have been bright times for the family, Natalie earning more than she had ever earned before, still writing with an enthusiasm that wouldn't quit, and now living at home, with Glen's military family allotment. Natalie even took a fresh interest in her daughter, although Jackie was still considered Amie's girl.

Weekends meant mother-daughter adventures beyond the neighborhood. One such adventure was at the CIO* Labor Hall, a concert by the famous African-American singer Paul Robeson.

Even Jackie had a small part in the program. On stage she recited a poem that began, "Take a Lincoln penny and hold it in your hand . . ." Afterward Mr. Robeson thanked Jackie and shook her hand, for Jackie, a treasured memory of her mother and the great black singer.

---

* Congress of International Organizations, years later combined with the American Federation of Labor (AFL).

But the interlude of well-being was brief indeed, and it would shortly all end in tragedy. Two months after Natalie began work at New Brighton, the Federal Bureau of Investigation—the FBI—had Natalie in its sights. On March 22 and April 4, damaging reports were distributed to five FBI offices, also to the State of Minnesota and to the Twin Cities Ordnance Plant. In the course of a few weeks, the FBI had accumulated a great deal of information.*

NATALIE BLANCH, aka Natalie Vail, Natalie J. Peake
Custodial Detention Summary Report
Subject's name appears on list of members of Victory Youth Club Branch of Young Communist League. She is a subscriber to the "Weekly Review," Young Communist League publication, and on December 7, 1942, donated blood as a member of the Young Communist League. She was born in White Earth, Minnesota, on April 23, 1914. She resides at the home of her mother, 2537 - 5th Avenue South, Minneapolis, and is employed by the Twin Cities Ordnance Plant at New Brighton, Minnesota.

Details

On April 1, 1943, a pretext telephone call was made to the Subject's mother, and it was ascertained that the Subject was presently residing at the home of her mother, and that she was employed at the Twin Cities Ordnance Plant.

Subject is employed as a machine operator at the Twin Cities Ordnance Plant, having been hired on February 10, 1943. Her social security number is 469-18-1986.

The nationalistic tendencies of this Subject are Communistic. A confidential source has advised that within the Communist Party Headquarters at 15 North 9th Street, Minneapolis, is a list believed to be the membership list of the Victory Youth

---

* The reports of March 22 and April 4, 1943, have been combined here into a single report. There were many repitions. Also, when the reports were unclassified in 2001, much information was deleted. On appeal by this author, the FBI informed her that the deletions had only to do with names of the informants and the special investigators. The author is doubtful, for the deletions were extensive.

Club Branch of the Young Communist League in Minneapolis. This list reflects the payment of dues by the various members, and in one instance reflects the payment of three "Anti-Fascist" assessments. Informant advised that the Subject's name appeared on a list entitled Victory Youth Club, which was observed in the meeting place of the Victory Youth Club at 2860 Chicago Avenue in Minneapolis. For two years prior to June, 1942, the Subject was on WPA, and as such, acted as librarian at the Minneapolis Labor School. This school bore the reputation of having among its teachers many Communists and followers of TROTSKY.

She was born at White Earth, Minnesota, of French-Indian descent. She was born on a Chippewa Reservation. Her father, FREDERICK PEAKE, was born at Crow Wing, Minnesota, and her mother, LOUISE PEAKE, was born in Wabasha, Minnesota. It is to be noted that this Subject was previously married, and has one child, age 5 years, who is being kept by the mother. The Subject attended Madison School and Central High School in Minneapolis, and attended the University of Minnesota for one year.

The records maintained in the office of the Minnesota Secretary of State reflect that the Subject signed the 1940 Communist Party Nominating petition.

A Custodial Detention Summary Report is being submitted on the Subject NATALIE BLANCH.

On June 16, 1943, under the signature of John Edgar Hoover, Director, the FBI sent a memorandum to the FBI Special War Policies Unit in Minneapolis: "It is recommended that the captioned individual [Natalie Blanch] be given consideration for custodial detention. . . ."

On July 3, a subsequent order, signed by John Edgar Hoover, read "re Natalie Blanch, with aliases Natalie Vail, Natalie J Peake: *You will prepare without delay a white card captioned as above and reflecting your investigative case file number for filing in your Confidential Custodial Detention Card File."*

At this late date, we can only surmise that Natalie was aware of her accumulating FBI file, perhaps also even knew about the

Custodial Detention Order. One day, when no one was really paying attention at home, she gathered together everything she had written—poems, essays, short stories—packed a small valise, and disappeared. Some days later Amie received a phone call from the Wauwatosa State Hospital in Wisconsin. Natalie had been brought there by the Milwaukee police, who had picked her up somewhere on the streets of the city, dazed and disheveled. The Wauwatosa hospital was specific. Someone must come immediately and fetch the young woman, for she was not a resident of Wisconsin. Emily was frantic. She phoned loyal friend Frances, who always seemed to be wise.

Presently, Emily and Frances were on their way to Wisconsin by train. What they found was a heavily drugged Natalie, with no possessions other than her purse. Natalie was released to them. They returned home by train under the watchful eye of the conductor. As they rode west in the night darkness, Emily repeated over and over, "Such a waste, such a wasted life."

Back in Minneapolis, there was little that could be done. The authorities had already been notified. Like her father a decade earlier, Natalie was hospitalized, declared incompetent, and sent to the Minnesota State Hospital at Anoka. The diagnosis: schizophrenia.

It became Emily's responsibility now to look after Natalie as best she could, better than Louise had been able to do for Fred when he was hospitalized. Once again, Frances accompanied Emily on the bus up to Anoka. This first visit turned out to be a shock and a revelation. They found Natalie in a ward of fifty beds with one nurse. All of the patients were absolutely docile, drugged it turned out. The nurse apologized to Emily. Had Emily phoned before coming, she would not have given Natalie her "morning medication." Then Natalie would have been in better shape to receive visitors.

But there was worse to come. Without consulting the family, the State of Minnesota transferred Natalie to the State Hospital at Rochester so that she could undergo a lobotomy. When Emily heard of this, she was beside herself. She immediately contacted Meridel LeSueur, who had never given up on Natalie and whom

Emily perceived as having good political connections. Meridel was even more agitated. A friend of hers had undergone such an operation and was now not much more than a vegetable. Thanks to Meridel's interference, the operation was canceled. Emily may not have agreed with Meridel's radical views, but for the rest of her life, she would acknowledge with gratitude Meridel's devotion to her sister.

After that near disaster, for as long as Natalie lived, Emily devised her own strategy. She occasionally sent presents to her sister, but more important, once she learned a nurse's name, she would frequently send the nurse little gifts—treats and trinkets—in the hope that Natalie would be treated with tenderness and with respect.

Emily in Uniform

It is very pretty here, everything is green. The ocean is very frisky, jumping up high and whirling itself into foamy mists. It is a beautiful green color with white foam.
—Emily at Palm Beach, October 28, 1944

Over the years, Amie had experienced much of life, the bad along with the good. She would change what she could and accept what she could not. Like Fred's breakdown, Natalie's too must be accepted. Amie now looked to the future in the lives of Emily and Jackie.

For Emily, acceptance was much more difficult. She was angry—not only at those whom she perceived to have led her sister astray, but also at her sister, as if Natalie had brought it all on herself. As they grieved together, mother and daughter talked about the trail that had led to this disaster, perhaps forgetting that little Jackie too had lost, and that she had greatly loved her mother. Like most children, Jackie listened and Jackie remembered. Even at age six, she would stand up and defend her mother when any negative word was spoken in her presence. It would take many, many years for Jackie to come to grips with the burdens these twin family tragedies had foisted on Emily and Amie.

Yet Emily was determined to move on in life, for that was her nature. Caught up in the wartime enthusiasm, she decided to join the military. The opportunity presented itself when recruiters for the Coast Guard came to town. In 1942 the Women's Coast Guard Reserve had come into being. It was promptly dubbed the SPARS, presumably to reflect its status as a "support" structure. But in fact SPAR stood for *Semper Paratus, Always Ready*, motto of the United States Coast Guard. Between 1942 and 1946, 10,000 women would serve in the SPARS, most of them trained initially at the Biltmore Hotel in Palm Beach, Florida. Once dubbed the "pink palace," this hotel was now a military establishment, with the entire interior—all 430 rooms—repainted in Coast Guard Blue.

In September 1944, Emily became a SPAR. During her 15 months in service, she would write extensive letters to her mother, faithfully once or twice a week. Amie saved all the letters, and years later Emily typed them together as one document.

It all began with a train ride to St. Louis, an entire day in the city, then a hot and dirty ride down to Palm Beach, sleeping in the top berth of a three-decker bunk, which Emily found quite amusing. Ensconced at the Biltmore, now the *ship*, Emily shared a room with five other young women. The first thing they did was to go swimming in the ocean, a new experience for Emily. She assured her mother that they really didn't swim, just jumped around in the waves, with a lifeguard watching. In the first days, Emily gathered seashells and seaweed, packed them up, and mailed them to Jackie. Emily was a *bootie*, a shipboard beginner. Her platoon had mess duty every other day—their assignment, to pour lemonade and milk. Then the classes began—history of the Coast Guard, along with the insignias and vocabulary, Red Cross and physical education, mostly swimming lessons in the pool. If one didn't know better, one would have thought the letters home were from a young girl at summer camp, away from her family for the first time.

When it came to the uniforms, this young woman from Minneapolis, who had never owned more than the most inexpensive of clothes, waxed positively eloquently: "Two play suits and nice shoes with 2-inch heels and bows on the front. The leather very good and they look great on my feet... nice terry cloth bathrobe and pink pajamas—all the clothing of very good material. My blue suit fits quite well and a blue hat to match... We don't have to wear stockings down here if our legs are tan enough." When, a month later, a new group of booties arrived, Emily and her pals became *boots:* a promotion to Seaman First Class and no more mess duty. Emily was assigned to advanced Yeoman School and the privilege of wearing a white hat. At school, she breezed through everything but the shorthand, which she hadn't used since high school. But that too came back, and by the end of November, Emily, now on top of it all, was promoted to Yeoman.

The SPAR Training Station, Palm Beach, 1944.

Thanksgiving, being also the second anniversary of the SPARS, was festival time at the Biltmore. It began with a parade of the SPARS in their blues and a regimental review on the converted golf course, then a magnificent Thanksgiving dinner on *shipboard* (the

Biltmore)—where the only thing missing was the turkey dressing—
a movie in the auditorium, and finally the birthday dance. "A friend
of Mary's brought a boy from Hopkins in for me. His name is Don
and he is a typical Minnesota boy with a healthy looking face. He
couldn't dance though, and I spent most of my time trying to teach
him. This always happens to me." A week later, on Sunday, Emily
and her friends went down to the Everglades: "...very different and
interesting, but this is definitely a tourist town. You should see these
people. They are the funniest I've ever seen. They look like retired
gangsters and they wear the funniest clothes, for instance, bright
green pants and pink coats. They get themselves tanned until they
are almost black."

Time to leave the idyllic Palm Beach, for Emily was now
assigned to the Coast Guard base in New Orleans. But first a leave
and a chance to spend Christmas with Amie and Jackie. What a
sensation Emily's arrival must have caused—the smart blue suit, the
blue winter hat, and the black leather shoes with the bows in front.
These were good times in the Peake household. Glen was fighting
the war in the Pacific, never really out of danger, but never that far
away in Jackie's world. A sensitive soul, as Natalie had once been,
he wrote poems and drew pictures for his stepdaughter. Besides,
his monthly family allotment check more than took care of her few
needs. And with Emily's allotment check going to her mother, for
the first time ever the household ran without worry. Louise had
time for her Na-gu-aub young women and was now also active in
the Gethsemane Altar Guild. She even joined the League of Women
Voters. Always, unless Jackie was in school, Amie had her in tow.
Jackie was comfortable with adults, who no doubt doted on "the
darling little half-breed." To anyone who would listen, Jackie was
pleased to announce, "My Amie is a Club Woman."

The months in New Orleans had a profound impact on Emily's
sense of identity. This was not so much reflected in her letters,
but rather spoken about in later years. At home, she had been
"something other, most likely an Indian." Here, where the Whites
may have been whiter and Blacks certainly were blacker, and
everyone seemed to know which was which, there was no question

as to who Emily Peake was. She was a "white," and it didn't hurt at all that she was in uniform.

At New Orleans, Emily moved into Coast Guard barracks and went to work for the Captain of the Port. This was office work, keeping up with the records of Coast Guard ships and sailors who were constantly moving in and out. In Emily's ten New Orleans months,

Emily home on leave, Christmas, 1944

she never got over the moisture, the rotting wood, the curious mix of people—"many negroes and variations, also some Mexicans and Indians and Spanish and French"—the termites, ants and cockroaches, and the poverty. "There doesn't seem to be a middle class as there is at home. There are only wealthy people and very poor people."

In addition to work, she enrolled in an evening zoology class at Tulane University, earning four credits. She even signed up for a ballet class. One evening she and her friend Dottie, with a couple of Air Corps lieutenants, made a tour of the French Quarter. For Emily, the most memorable part of the evening was watching little black boys tap dancing on the street. Wrote Emily, no mean tap dancer herself, "You should have seen those little feet fly."

By March it became clear that the war was winding down, at least the European part. Emily was already thinking of home and the future. "Have your heard anything from Uncle Niles* lately... My hair resembles the old mop in the back hall, only a little darker in color... Jackie, I received the pretty robin and I like him very much. He sat on my desk at work yesterday. I went to school again last night and saw some more cardinals and some mockingbirds."

On Easter Sunday "we donned our Easter whites and went to church, an Episcopal one. We walked around and let all the people look at us, for the white is rather startling. Everybody stared at us and I thought we looked pretty nice." On other weekends there were concerts—Jascha Heifetz and Jose Iturbe—a performance by the New Orleans Opera, and sports—swimming in the base pool, bicycling on the levees, and tennis with equipment borrowed from the "Morale Department." Emily was even seized by a bit of spring fever:

> *A friend of mine from my Zoology class is coming to loan me his book. He is a very amusing little sailor with a big shock of curly hair in front of his sailor cap. He comes from Georgia and got shot in the leg, collecting souvenirs while on armed guard duty on Saipan. Not only that, but he got a Captain's Mast (sort of a punishment, an easy one though) and sent back to the states. He wasn't supposed to be souvenir hunting on that island. His name is Sheehan.*
>
> *Springtime has a different flavor down here. The earth doesn't sleep very long nor have a blanket of snow. Many of the trees have green leaves all winter long, but some are breaking out into new garb. On the way to school at night there are lots of birds that chirp and chirp. Tulane has a*

---

* Niles Beaupre at White Earth, Louise's brother.

beautiful campus, very spacious and green. They have two colleges, one for the boys and one for the girls, called Newcomb. Some of the girls in my class are graduates of Newcomb. They think it is very odd to have classes with boys and can't understand how it is to have classes with them. Ever since 8th grade they are separated and I think they behave very peculiarly in the presence of the opposite sex, as if they fell off the moon or something.

Emily took note of President Roosevelt's death on April 12. "We all felt very sad about it. It was too bad it happened so soon." At the end of the month Emily passed her exam and became a Petty Officer. On May 8, all of the whistles of New Orleans were blown to celebrate VE Day [Victory in Europe]. But there was no celebration in the Port Authority Captain's office, just more work to be done. Japan was a long way from surrendering. "We'll be lucky if it is all over by Christmas." So said the Captain. Still, it was all in the air. Little by little, the Allies were taking back the Pacific Ocean. Soon after VE Day, the Philippine Islands, seized so ignominiously by the Japanese back in 1942, were retaken by United States forces. When United States forces seized the Japanese island of Okinawa, just a hop and a skip from the Japanese mainland, one waited daily for the surrender. But it just wouldn't come. Then on August 6 an atomic bomb was dropped on the city Hiroshima. Two days later the Soviet Union declared war on Japan. Another atomic bomb was dropped August 9, this time on Nagasaki.

End of the War

I was sitting on a little canvas chair on the bridge, watching another Coast Guard Cutter through the binoculars and chattering with a fellow from Wisconsin. Someone gave a burst on the ship's horn. We were wondering what it meant when someone came up the side saying 'The war is over.' We could hear shouts of joy coming from the mess hall. One of the fellows grabbed the signal flags and signaled the other ship: the war is over from the Boutwell.

Back from the other ship: WE KNOW HURRAY

—Emily on board the Coast Guard Cutter *Boutwell* on the lower Mississippi, August 14, 1945

It would be another three months before Emily was discharged from the Coast Guard, and if the Port Authority office had been busy during the war, the pace had now become absolutely frenetic. On top of that, Emily's boss was immediately discharged. Emily was assigned to his job, at the same time training a new SPAR into her old job. Seven hundred files had to be checked "to see that they are absolutely accurate and ready for immediate discharge." Too often there were hitches of one kind or another.

This morning a man was in who was about to be discharged. His name was Zambrinski. . . . However, no one could find his health records. . . . He was very sad because they had stricken him from the original list and he was having to wait for a duplicate from Washington. Somehow or other he came over to my desk and told me his woes. I told him to calm down and have a chair and I'd look around for his health record. Well, I found it in the sick bay file, which sometimes happens. When I showed it to him, he had the happiest face I've ever seen. The first thing he said was that he would take me on a big drunk. I guess I must have made a very funny face at this most generous offer because the whole office broke out into loud laughter. Then he said he would send me something from home, which turned out to be in St. Paul.

Two weeks later Emily wrote, "I received a nice bottle of Honeysuckle Cream Cologne from the St. Paul Emporium and a very pretty hanky. I didn't really expect to get anything. It made me very happy."

In October Emily wheedled a few days' liberty out of the Personnel Officer and took the train to Tulsa, Oklahoma, where Aunt Emily lived. Emily Peake, Papa's closest sibling, who graduated from Carlisle a year after Papa, winning every honor Carlisle had to offer, who went on to get a teaching degree, then worked in the Indian Service until she married and moved to Tulsa, who outlived two husbands, both Indian lawyers, now looked to her namesake Emily as the Peake onto whom she would pass her mantle. For five days the two Emilys sat together while Aunt Emily told tales of her mother—Keche-ogemah (Isabel Peake Schneider)—of their family dodem (the crane)—of the early White Earth years, and of Papa, the best orator at Carlisle and the fiercest defender of Indian justice anywhere.

By the time Emily bid goodbye to Aunt Emily, a new mindset was evolving. On the outside nothing had changed. Emily was still the fun-loving, outgoing, joyous young woman whom her family, friends, and colleagues all loved. But deep inside some latent Ojibwe blood had been stirred. Emily Louise Peake's life was definitely a work in progress.

Reclaiming Ojibwe Roots

It was a treat when I took my American Indian outfits and paraphernalia
to school. I enjoyed telling my classmates about them and it felt good,
jabbing at the prejudice.

—Emily's niece Jackie

Peacetime! What a luxury, what hope, what promise for the future!

On November 30, 1945, after serving fifteen months in the Coast Guard, Emily was discharged at St. Louis, Missouri. Two days later she arrived in Minneapolis, wearing her blue military uniform. One can only imagine the excitement, for Amie, for Emily, and for nine-year-old Jackie. Adieu was home!

Emily wasted not a day before charging into her future. By the second of January she was enrolled at the University of Minnesota, ready to complete her last two years of college. All this thanks to the "GI Bill of Rights," passed by Congress in June of 1944. Not only would the GI Bill pay for Emily's tuition, it would also provide for books and maintenance. If Emily wasn't thinking about this when she joined the SPARS, it certainly must have become clear long before she left the service.

But life must be more than just books. In Emily's world, people and projects were second nature. She had long ago given up the hope of studying ballet, but with the dancing skills she already had acquired—tap, mostly self-taught, plus the few ballet lessons in New Orleans—why not *teach* dancing. Just three blocks away from home was the Elliott Park Neighborhood House, a "settlement house" where children in this less privileged neighborhood could find activities, friends, and if needed, some extra adult guidance. Jackie was already well connected at Elliott Park House. Thus it was she who first introduced Emily to this great old green mansion with gables, where children's voices could be heard seven days a week.

Emily loved children passionately, from adorable babies to agreeable ten-year-olds, even to not-so-agreeable teenagers. It made no difference; Emily could always come through. She certainly wasn't blind to race, for *it* is most often visible at first glance, but she had the knack for instantly seeing beyond. The Elliott Park children were as mixed in race as they were in age.

What better place to have a dance school. So reasoned Emily, and so the classes began—Saturday mornings ballet and taps. One might say it was at Elliott Park House that Volunteer Emily first honed her skills as a beggar, skills for which she would become famous in later years. None of the children had either tap shoes or ballet slippers, let alone ballet tutus. At first Emily scrounged for the shoes, using her own funds to buy taps and slippers at the Salvation Army, after arranging by phone to have put aside any that came in. But how much better if there were new shoes and new slippers. Emily began to appear at board meetings, and in her own disarming way she badgered the board—money for taps, slippers, tulle, and small subsidies for the occasional recitals. At the suggestion that recitals be a source of modest funding for the classes, Emily was adamant. Not only would dance recitals be offered free, but refreshments would always be served. One can imagine her taking a cue from her own childhood—those theater performances in the hot attic, where penny candy was the draw.

Natalie was still at Rochester State Hospital. If either Emily or Amie ever did visit her, it was a day-long train ride, forth and back, with hardly an hour in between, usually to bring new clothes, for Natalie's clothes and personal possessions disappeared with amazing frequency. At this late date, even Jackie does not know how much her mother was aware of her situation, whether she understood her condition or was even aware of her loved ones back at home.

In May of 1946, a short story titled "Ollie," by Natalie Blanch, appeared in *New Masses*. This was a leftist literary monthly of some renown. The editorial board included literary giant Howard Fast. Among the contributing editors were W.E.B. Dubois, Rockwell Kent, Paul Robeson, and indeed Meridel LeSueur. "Ollie" was probably the last piece of writing Natalie ever completed before her 1943 breakdown, the only piece that did not disappear on her fateful escape to Milwaukee. No doubt by that time the manuscript was already in Meridel's hands. Certainly Meridel's influence is present in this vignette about a young factory woman, facing her thirtieth birthday, living with her widowed mother, who is keeping the household together by hook or crook, a young woman with little hope for the future except in marriage to a young man who is studying to be a machinist, a young woman who essentially betrays his trust even as he betrays hers. "Ollie" is a well-written classic short story, but with the added proletarian twist, which made it suitable for *New Masses*. One can imagine Meridel's delight when she delivered the periodical to Natalie's family. To this day, Jackie treasures it above all other mementos of her mother's unfulfilled and tragic life.

In the first years after World War II, years when Meridel LeSueur's writing career was stifled and eventually eclipsed by the politics of the time, oddly enough she turned increasingly to the Peake women—mother, daughter, and granddaughter. Certainly they were all tied together through Natalie, but there was more. Emily, who years earlier had almost denied her Ojibwe roots, now wanted very much to explore them and to bring Jackie along in her quest.

Beginning in 1946, and continuing through 1949, always in June, Amie and Emily and Jackie took the train north to White Earth. On the weekend nearest June 14, White Earth celebrated the 1868 arrival of the first two hundred Ojibwe from Gull Lake, whose descendents now outnumbered the founders many times over. Anniversary for Amie meant homecoming—Peakes and Beaupres by the dozens, and more recently the Boutwells also. Nita, daughter of brother Niles Beaupre, had married a Boutwell. And like Grandma Schneider's farm on Snyder Lake a generation earlier, and like Amie's home in Minneapolis, the Boutwell farm was a center of hospitality. Even better, the farm held a magic of its own, especially for a child like Jackie who was raised on city streets. These June homecomings meant games, food, talk and more talk, dancing, costumes, and always the drums—those wonderful drums whose insistent cadences called forth the Anishinabe beginnings. More often than not, Meridel LeSueur also came along. Perhaps she too was looking for roots—to her own lost heritage, to connections she could barely define.

The Graduate

In 1947 Emily was awarded a Bachelor of Arts degree from the University of Minnesota, with a major in psychology and minors in history and political science. She promptly found work at General Mills, that same corporation for which dear Papa had labored twenty years earlier. The position was as secretary in the advertising department, in downtown Minneapolis, a pleasant walk from home. The work was a breeze and the pay competitive.

Years later, when asked what she learned in her two years with General Mills, Emily would invariably reply, "to eat oatmeal." It seems that the food research staff at General Mills had undertaken an experiment with white rats. Over some specified period, one group was fed exclusively on Cheerios, a second group was fed on Wheaties, and a third group on oatmeal. When the results were evaluated, it turned out that the Cheerios rats had acquired yellow tails, the Wheaties rats had become very fat, and the oatmeal rats had grown strong and healthy. So reported Emily.

What made the General Mills experience all worthwhile, far beyond Emily's initial expectations, was getting to know a colleague, Jacqueline Daveluy Raasch, a "war bride" from Paris. The friendship between these two women was immediate and long lasting. No wonder, for Emily had always had a dream—to visit France. Perhaps this longing came through Grandma Carrie—Caroline Beaupre, who once was a Le Havre, who spoke with a "French" accent and dressed "like Paris," the mother who addressed her own daughter Louise as *Mon Amie*, the grandmother whom Emily barely knew, yet the grandmother who represented all that was romantic and much that was beautiful.

Outside the workplace, Emily insisted on speaking French with Jacqueline, in hopes of improving her accent and increasing her vocabulary. When Jacqueline's mother, Mme. Daveluy, visited from Paris, Emily was the designated American she should meet first. Out of this encounter came the invitation from Mme. Daveluy: "Come to Paris, stay with us, and, if you choose, take some courses at the Sorbonne." It was an invitation too enticing to refuse. Thus, in the fall of 1950, Emily left General Mills and set off for Paris, her goal to spend six months at the Sorbonne doing graduate work in abnormal psychology—the subject choice no doubt driven by Emily's desire, and her fear, that mental illness lurked in her family genetic pool.

On the Way

Mes Amies . . . I've got to get to the ship in a couple of hours and between that time and now go out and mail this, buy an ironing cord, some cigarettes [for M. Daveluy], and I guess that's all. . . . Tiens, this is the last letter you will get in English, so that's why it is so long.
—Emily Peake to Jacqueline and friends
from New York, October 26, 1950

On the nineteenth of October, Emily boarded the train for the first stop on her journey to Paris, namely, Chicago. It must not have been an easy farewell at Minneapolis's Great Northern Station. Jackie and Amie would be alone once again, only it would be a bit different now. When Emily went off to the Coast Guard, Jackie was an adorable and adaptable seven-year-old, a joy for any grandmother to raise. Now at thirteen, Jackie may still have been adorable, but as a budding adolescent, not necessarily so adaptable. From all that happened later, we can surmise that Jackie once again felt the ache of abandonment within her fragile family. Probably

Emily comforted her, "Remember, it's only for six months." This was a promise that would soon be broken.

Emily spent the weekend in Chicago with Frances Green Anderson, who was now working in this great, totally American city.

There was a curious, and indeed quite wonderful, aspect of Emily. In friendships, she invariably gave more than she received. Besides that, she could never let go of a friend. First it was the Belladettes—Midge, Iney, and Dixie—then Frances, later the General Mills "kids"—Jacqueline, Simone, Juta, Nancy, and Suzie. To all of these Emily wrote long, descriptive letters over the two and a half years she would be away. As time went by, there would be dozens more such friends. Emily's one regret, often spoken of in later years, was that she lost contact with her Coast Guard colleagues, who had become such dear friends in the months they were all together.

Chicago: Four nights and three days, with more adventures than one might expect in a week, all on foot or by streetcar and elevated. First a stop at the French Consulate to pick up a visa. It was after 4:00 and the Consulate was closed. That night, dinner at Frances's and talking until late into the night. Friday morning, another trip to the Consulate, this time with success, a look-around at Marshall Field's, then a two-mile walk along Lake Michigan. "The sun and the air felt good." That evening, the Ballet Russe de Monte Carlo. "Les Sylphides, which had some wonderful Chopin music, Bluebird, Romeo and Juliet with all that lovely Tchaikovsky music and the third act to Raymonda. All very, very good." On Saturday, with Frances, down to the famous Maxwell Street—

where this rather interesting looking colored vendor stopped us and told us the funniest story. He was very dark, but had rather slanting eyes and a pointed beard. He was quite young and really had quite a story. He grabbed me by the coat and said, "Wait a minute, I've something for you." Then he grabbed up a funny looking old shrunken head with some matted hair attached and proceeded to tell us the most wild tale of how he had gone all over Europe and America and finally in South America found this head,

which had been shrunken by some vicious Indians who at the same time had
discovered a wonderful perfume distilled from the petals of rare flowers, all
of which he had for me at 25 cents a bottle.

The young women resisted the perfume, but bought ten pairs of silk stockings for $1.00 and later discovered that not even two of them were of a pair, which caused such a burst of laughter that they were almost crying. Emily had her fortune told by a Gypsy woman who said she was from Minnesota and could have been "any one of the old women on the reservation," then to Hull House for an informal tour, on the way back stopping at a Mexican shop that had such beautiful "hand carved coffee tables, hammered aluminum masks and an endless variety of little things" that Emily and Frances stayed almost an hour, finally, to a Greek restaurant for dinner and back to Frances's apartment on the "horrible elevated—I dislike them very much." Still time for an English movie, "Last Holiday," which Emily expected to be a comedy, but turned out to be very sad. On Sunday, another full day, beginning with the Museum of Science and Industry, where Emily saw herself as viewed on television, rode an elevator down to a simulated coal mine, and afterward sat through an old film with Mary Pickford and Lionel Barrymore. "They were both very cute in those days." That night, a play called "The Innocents," where "a couple of spooks come back to try to gain control of the souls of two children. The children in the play were very good, in fact it was all very good. I enjoyed it."

On to New York: After an overnight train ride, on which Emily "felt I had slept in a washing machine all night," she arrived at Grand Central Station, where Aunt Maude, the wife of dear Uncle George—Chief Little Moose—brought a bouquet of flowers and scooped Emily into her arms. Of all Emily's aunts and uncles—and there were many—Uncle George was the most familiar and no doubt the most beloved. Whatever difficulties there might have been over the years between Papa and his brother George, the summer interludes at the Wisconsin Dells, with little Emily on stage, dressed in her Chippewa dress and holding hands with Chief Little Moose, had forged a permanent bond between them. But

Uncle George was no longer impresario for Indian performances and certainly no longer a dancer himself. He was not well at all, especially his heart. It was Aunt Maude, equally beloved from the Wisconsin Dells summers, who would show Emily New York, beginning at the station—breakfast at Child's, then to Rockefeller Center and Radio City Theater for a performance of the dancing Rockettes, afterward lunch at the Shanghai Royal, with "some good chow mein," then into a taxi for a drive on Fifth Avenue and through Central Park. The next day Emily was on her own, first to the "Chicago station" to pick up her trunk and take it to the pier. After that, down to Wall Street to exchange money for French francs. "The first place I went to offered 300 for a dollar, but I kept going to every bank on that old money bags street until I found one that would give 377 for a dollar. This I took. . . . On this street in front of the New York Stock Exchange was . . . a rather rough looking character shouting 'Nya - ya olde bum- y ain't no good.' These people here have a very funny way of speaking. They say *oi* like *droivah* for driver (not *oi* like in French though)." Still time to drop into Trinity Church, where a Bach organ concert was in progress, and even look in on a museum that was "the building where the first Continental Congress met in 1765 and where George Washington was later inaugurated president."

October 27, 1950: "Here I am sitting out in the ocean about 500 miles out and on the way. I am not sick at all and have had a wonderful time so far."

Woman of the World

An American in Paris

For the first time in my life I was not an 'Indian,' not 'part Indian,'
not even 'white.' I was an American and what a wonderful feeling that was.
—Emily, speaking of her time in Europe*

Out of the many, many letters Emily wrote home from Europe, there comes through a very strong picture of her love affair with Paris, with France, the French culture, and not the least, the French people. To begin with, she arrived well prepared. More than a decade after high school, her French was still with her, and ten days on a French ocean liner where almost no one was speaking English brought it all to the surface. To her own amazement, the sociable American Emily discovered that the French language just flowed from her lips.

Emily's Paris months turned out to be an idyll, well chronicled in her letters home. She was living with M. and Mme. Daveluy, attending lectures at the Sorbonne, along with courses in Psychopathology at the Hospital of St. Anne, hopping over to England for Christmas, Easter on the English Channel, all in addition to weekly Sunday excursions with the Daveluys: the Concergerie, "the place where Marie Antoinette and the others were held before they went you know where"; "Sainte Chapelle, which was . . . the most beautiful thing I have ever seen. . . I think I could have stayed there an hour just looking at the windows. Most are Bible stories and tales of the saints' lives. I wish I knew more about the saints"; the Chamber of Deputies, "a nice red-plush-seated

---

* Phone interview with Frances Green Anderson, August 2001.

113

room . . . in a semicircle with the most liberal group on the left (Communists) and the most conservative on the right. . . . There are several parties here—Communists, Socialists, Christian Democrats, and the conservatives, of which Pleven is the spokesman, also the DeGaullists. The day I visited nothing much was going on. However, I did notice that many more members sat on the left than on the right. There was a short but firey argument between Pleven and Duclos (Communist) over the fact that the radio is supported with tax money and it gives out propaganda for the right. . . . I'm sure it would be the other way around if the Communists had control. These men are very good speakers in spite of the fact that they get quite excited and the debate turns into more or less a brawl. . . . I am hoping to return again before the elections in June. That should be exciting as the political feeling is very strong here between right and left (the DeGaullists, almost a military fascist form of government, versus the Communist left) . . ."; St. Germaine, "where Louis the 14th was born, also where Mary Stuart, Queen of Scots, lived while she was Queen of France for a while . . ."; even a wax museum with "wax images of Marie Antoinette in prison, Napoleon, all the Louis (or many of them), Joan of Arc, the life of Jesus . . . a room all of mirrors and colored lights . . . something like a palace out of the 'Tales of Scheherazade'"; "the old *stade* (stadium), where the Christians were eaten by the lions . . ."; a visit to a Paris cemetery, where Emily discovered a tomb with the name de Beaupre. "Mme. Daveluy tells me it is the name of a noble family here and that I should try to find where they live. Maybe we have some relatives still here. Do you know where the Beaupres came from? Also what was Grandma Carrie's maiden name and where did her family come from?"*—and much, much more.

---

* In Emily's last years, she would embark on a quest to discover the roots of Caroline Le Havre Beaupre (Grandma Carrie). Accompanied by niece Jackie, she would travel to Texas and Mississippi, visiting court houses and historical societies. No tie was ever found to the "noble" de Beaupres of Paris, but the Le Havres—that was another story. This quest would be remembered by Jackie as the healing of old wounds and the culmination of her bonding with Emily, a bonding that would transcend even death.

Emily's letters to Amie and young Jackie were so detailed, so comprehensive, with so many historical references, it is obvious she was engaging in an effort not only to educate, but more important, to broaden the vision of her mother and her niece. Always Emily was thinking of home—frequently sending little gifts and pictures, especially to Jackie. On May 21 she wrote, "Jackie, do you still have your braces or did they take them off. . . . Amie, I hope you picked up some weight. Don't get too thin and be sure not to worry as I will be home soon now. I went to see about a reservation yesterday, but he said I had plenty of time."

One can only imagine the chagrin at home when Emily went on to write, "I sent in the application for the summer school in Vienna—it sounds so good. I will have a chance to learn German quite well too. This is really a wonderful opportunity for me and I must make the best of it." For Jackie, this was not good news. She may well have put her annoyance into words: "But Adieu said it would only be for six months."

Vienna, City of Adventure

Tonight I am in Vienna, and I must say that I sometimes wonder what on earth I am doing so far away and in such a strange country. . . . I was very sad to leave [Paris] and had difficulty in carrying on any sensible conversation for the last three days.
                    —Emily in a letter home, early July 1951

The Austria that greeted Emily that summer was an "occupied" nation. It had been united with Germany during the Second World War. Thus, it was under the control of the four great powers that six years earlier had defeated Germany: the United States, England, France, and the Soviet Union. Such a small country, such a grand capital, and all so curiously divided—four *zones* of occupation, each occupied by military forces belonging to one of

115

the four great powers, Vienna likewise divided into four *sectors*, plus an international sector in the center of the city, with a monthly changing of the guard, all under an elaborate governing board consisting of the Allied Council, the Executive Committee, the Allied Secretariat, the Directorates, Sub-Committies, Working Partites, and an Inter-Allied Command.

In exploring Emily's Viennese sojourn—two full years during this postwar occupation—one comes upon several puzzles. The first is how she came to be hired by the Secretariat of the four-power council. Many of Emily's letters are missing, either destroyed by Emily herself or simply lost in the hectic family years that followed. Probably Emily went to Vienna to explore a summer language school opportunity. Yet on July 17 she went to work for the four-power occupation Secretariat as a clerk secretary, earning more than she had ever earned at home. The U.S. State Department, Emily's ultimate employer, agreed to deduct an allotment each month and send it home to her mother. With this amount, Amie could run her modest household and provide for Jackie. Yes, Emily had broken her promise to Jackie, but that couldn't be helped. A paying job in Europe was just too delectable an opportunity. Still, that did not prevent Emily from registering for both German and Russian courses at the Berlitz School of languages. Using the last of her Veteran's Education funds, she had enough for classes five nights a week. It was here, at the school, that Emily met the American Tony, who would become her constant friend for the entire Vienna sojourn. What began as a collegial relationship in class soon evolved into a serious friendship. For almost two years Tony and Emily dated regularly at least once a week, principally concerts and sightseeing. *

From the very first moment, life in Vienna suited Emily's adventurous spirit to a tee. She promptly rented a little room in the home of a family Marchhart, whose roots were in Romania. Also living at the Marchharts was the family Essmann, Jewish refugees

---

* How do we know all this? U.S. Army Intelligence documents. In her letters home Emily never mentioned Tony's last name. And much later, in documents furnished to this author by U.S. Army Intelligence, Tony's name was blackened out.

from Hungary, once very prosperous, having somehow survived the Nazi occupation, then fleeing to Austria in the wake of a Communist pogrom, now awaiting more adequate housing. Such a congenial bunch they all were. The Essmanns were ice skating enthusiasts, and they taught Emily how to "dance" on skates. Sundays now she was also riding horseback at a riding school. She started out on *Max*, "pink color and kind of a big pony," then graduated to *Schwan*, who became her favorite. Once Emily found some popcorn in the American PX. She made it for the Marchharts, who hadn't tasted popcorn for ten years. Wrote Emily,

> When the first panful came off the fire, they shouted with glee, 'Real Romanian Koukourouts.' But I held my own, saying, 'No, it's really American. The Indians were the first to find it.'....Then I made some for the Essmanns, and they too said 'Real Hungarian Koukourouts.' All of these times I was quietly but firmly objecting and saying that these were really American products, but I don't think any of them believed me.

In January Emily attended the annual American-Austrian Ball with her friend Tony, who brought along two Austrian friends, Rudy and Peter. After borrowing a "lovely blue dress," which Frau Essmann altered, and then posing for a photo, Emily was ready for the ball.

> We found a taxi very near here on the corner (the taxis here are something like a 1918 model, no, more 1928, to be honest). When we arrived, the ball had already begun. It was at the Musikvereinsalle, which is a big concert house, a lovely building done in deep burgundy and gold colors with huge chandeliers and lovely paintings....When we arrived, they were playing some lovely Viennese waltz music, so off I went with Rudy to try dancing the Wiener Waltz with a real Viennese (ein echter Wiener). Believe me, it was an experience. The room was very crowded, the music wonderful and we were off in a whirl—and a real whirl it was. No sooner would we take two full whirls when wham! we bumped into someone. The music got faster and faster and we twirled faster and faster, legs, arms, pointed elbows, heads all at once (reminded me of Picasso's "Guernice"). What Rudy

was doing with his feet now I had no idea. Finally, as we weren't bumping into our usual number of people, he just picked me up and we twirled

around for what seemed to me to be another hour or so. Finally the music ended, the floor and lights became a little more stable, Rudy bowed very politely, kissed my hand and said with much pride, "That is the real Wienerwaltz!"... The next Wiener Waltz I did with Tony, who does it American style; this I could do. I'll learn it yet, though—that Wienerwaltz! The rest of the evening was spent dancing in turn with my three friends, who were already rested between the dances and in fine form, while you-know-who was pretty dead by 4:00 A.M.

Emily in Vienna, ready for the Ball, January 1952

These Vienna letters—so filled with detailed descriptions of people, operas, ballets, and places visited—say very, very little about Emily's work. What we learn is that Emily visited Florence, made a short visit to Paris, toured Berchtesgaden in spring, and promised to be home soon. To Amie and Jackie, she wrote, "I have a ticket to come home on the *Liberte* the 28th of October, *this year*, unless something happens sooner."

A Secretary in the Secretariat

*Like a bunch of wolves groveling over the carcass of poor little Austria
and taking a bite out of each other at the same time.*
—Emily's description of the
Allied Commission, June 5, 1952

Perhaps for the moment Emily truly believed she would be home in October. She began to write much more openly about the men and women with whom she worked, and how they related to one another, even as the East-West Cold War was taking hold. To her mother she wrote, "Don't worry about the Russians. They are very good to us here, that is, in the place where we work, very friendly. However, as far as politics go, they don't love us very much, naturally."

In another letter from that time she wrote,

> *Here is a little sample of some of our more immediate dealings with the Russians. They are really ordinary people just like everybody else. The other day I was at a Directorate meeting taking the notes (Minutes). Across from me sat the Soviet member, a Mr. Kirsanov (which I think means something like "Mr. Cherry"). He is a small serious little man who wore a brown suit, had a rather browned face and sparse hair. Beside him sat two interpreters. One interprets from English to Russian and vice versa and the other French-Russian. They are both young. Well, this Directorate is kind of confused as a whole anyway. Speaking three different languages tends to lend to the confusion. They were discussing the signing of three sets of Minutes, those of 4 September, 15 October and 20 October. After the discussion had finished, the Soviet man said, "But what about the Minutes of 20 October? I haven't heard anything about them." And the Chairman, who is a real English pumpkin head, replied, "We have been discussing*

them for the past fifteen minutes." Nobody thought that unusual or funny
except myself and those two Russian devils sitting across from me. They
got themselves behind their man so he couldn't see them and just got all
red laughing silently. I of course had to face the man and wanted badly to
escape, but couldn't.

In April Emily moved into her own apartment. "I do have some
news to tell you now. I have a new government apartment. It is very
cute. It has a living room, bedroom, kitchen and bathroom, all for
me. I was sorry to leave Frau Marchhart, but she understands. . ."

The Four Power Occupation Commission
Emily in the back corner, 1952

Clearly Emily was more than comfortable in her cosmopolitan
life. A ski trip to Zell-am-See, beyond Salzburg, a weekend in Wachau,
"one of the most beautiful areas in Austria," an adventure in Türnitz,
deep in the Russian zone, including a day-long bicycle trip through
the countryside, other weekend excursions to Linz and Mödling,
bicycling in the mountains, by train to Yugoslavia, a heart-wrenching
visit to Dachau, and still another sentimental journey to Paris.

But always back to Vienna, where life never stood still.

I must tell you about my visit to the Parliament here. The Parliament is
a lovely building on the outside. . . . On the lawn in front of the building

stands a big statue of Minerva, the Goddess of Wisdom. I have a friend who says they should have her inside where they could use a little extra wisdom—couldn't we all. I must tell you that I had a special ticket from the Baron who is a liaison between the Allied Powers and Austria and therefore comes to visit our office often. He is a very nice old man and was very good to get me a place in the Diplomat box, where I could see and hear very well. Inside the Parliament is just about what you would expect it to be. It is on the order of the French Chambre des Deputies but doesn't seem as cozy to me as the French Parliament. The color scheme is brown leather and green. Around the wall are big statues of Father Rhine and Mother Danube holding up pillars and balancing doorways on their heads. (Father Rhine doesn't look too happy.) . . . For the first ¾ of an hour it was very dull as finance laws and ordinances were read, one after the other. Then, just before everybody dropped completely off, came the Communist delegate

**Emily and Colleagues at the Commmission
Offices, 1953**

to the microphone. He gave a firey speech of ½ hour that had the whole house awakened with other representatives jumping up and down in their seats and shouting remarks, but he had the microphone. . . . The speech was directed against the Marshall Plan and was entitled "Austria Aids America Instead of America Aids Austria." He said that the Marshall Plan has only brought inflation and that Austria had lost 3 thousand million schillings to America during 1951. He said the government was sold out to the Americans. This brought shouts of "and who is sold out to the Russians?"

from the floor. This of course was the most exciting part of the meeting. However, the man was a very good speaker. They don't get quite as mad at each other as they do in the French Parliament. There it is possible to come to blows with the fists. Here they just blow words at each other, as can only be done in German. I stayed until he had finished as I knew the rest wouldn't be so exciting. Then I made a dramatic exit by falling out of the Diplomat box, not really falling, just sort of stumbling over something that was in the way. *

And in the same letter:

The most recent of my adventures was our invitation to the Russian Embassy here. We, together with the French and English at the Secretariat, were invited by the Russians to attend a showing of a movie called The Gala Concert ... in a private showing at their embassy. We all accepted eagerly as we were most anxious to see just what the embassy looked like. . . . Inside it is all white marble with coral marble pillars, and great chandeliers. We were met in the hall by the Russian Deputy High Commissioner and another Russian General. We see them every Friday, so we know them quite well now. . . . We were ushered into another lovely room that had silken blue tapestries all around the walls. It too was in white marble with a large chandelier. We were offered vodka, red wine, champagne, caviar sandwiches and many other delicacies. It is very amusing here. We converse among ourselves— people from four different countries—in the funniest German you ever heard. I am sure the Austrian waitresses must have gotten a big kick out of us. . . . After the movie we were again served with the same delicious tidbits we had been offered before. I think everyone enjoyed it and it was very nice of the Russians to invite us. No one would think we were the same group of people who insult each other around a conference table.

---

* In 1947 Secretary of State George C. Marshall called for U.S. assistance in restoring the economic infrastructure of Europe. The nations of western Europe responded favorably. The resulting Economic Cooperation Act of 1948 restored European agricultural and industrial productivity. Credited with preventing famine and political chaos, the plan later earned General Marshall a Nobel Peace Prize. Those nations under Soviet domination were given the opportunity to participate, but under Soviet pressure they declined.

What a contrast to these glittering Viennese interiors were her mother's disturbing letters from home. Amie was now sixty-six years old, raised in a different time and culture. She found it

Lunch at the Office, Emily and colleagues, 1952

increasingly difficult to make any sort of decision regarding her granddaughter. Yet she dared not plead for Emily's return. Even so, Emily somehow had to be brought into the mix. Jackie's three years at Phillips Junior High School had been just plain unhappy. Counseled Emily from the other side of the ocean,

> *About the University High School. That is of course a very good high school and, if [Jackie] wants to go there, I see no reason (outside of the money, which I hope we have enough of) why she shouldn't. I think it would be much better for her than Central and she is more likely to meet interesting children. However, I can't say anything bad about my alma mater and it certainly is much better than Phillips. Children who come through Phillips without becoming juvenile delinquents are really darn good little kids with good characters. Central has a much better reputation.*

In September 1952, Jackie did enter Central High School. On October 28, as scheduled, the *Liberte* sailed from France, but Emily was not among the passengers. Her Secretariat position had been extended yet another year. Letters that might have explained this development and softened the blow to Amie and Jackie are now missing. To be fair to Emily, it may well be that her salary—much of which she sent home—was so substantial that she hated to give it up for the unknown that would face her once she returned. Most likely the question of Tony also played a part in Emily's indecision. Any future with Tony would have to include Amie and Jackie. Was Tony up to being a partner in Emily's family responsibilities? Probably not.

In any case, Emily was always bent on improving herself, and for the moment *language* was her goal. Her Veteran's education benefits had run out, but no matter. Emily was now fluent in both French and German. Yet she was determined to master the Russian language also. Her friend Tony was still struggling with German, but he followed along just the same. Together they found one Professor Christinsky, who gave weekly classes. One night he invited them to his home.

> *You know these people are really Russians and they made the most wonderful food, all kinds of cakes and tasty things to eat. . . . Then they moved all the furniture back in their living room, which really isn't very big, and made a place for us to dance. The father, my Russian teacher, can do a wonderful polka and he taught me how to do a Ukrainian dance. The part of the girl is really very simple, but the man's part is difficult. He gets way down and kicks his legs out in front of him. . . . Tony tried to do it and broke his belt. He is so funny.*

In April another party.

> *On Sunday my Russian professor invited Tony and me to his house, where we had the most wonderful Russian food. A big high sort of sponge cake made like a tower and topped with some wonderful cream. Then there was Paskha, which is more difficult to explain, but delicious. It looks like cream cheese but tastes like ice cream without the coldness. It is filled with fruits and dates and is eaten with this sweet bread. We had some Vodka, too. I drank a little bit and it was very good. There were only Russian people there,*

*one former Countess, and a lady whose husband has been a prisoner of the
Russians for thirteen years. Isn't that terrible? They spoke only Russian and
even though I understand only a little, I could follow quite well.*

Fractured Trust

It was not long after the Russian party that Emily received the news.
She was informed by the Secretariat that her contract would not be
renewed. Perhaps it was time. Emily had been away now almost
two and a half years. In this time Jackie had grown from an adorable
child to an unhappy adolescent, desperately in need of the kind of
parenting that only Emily could give. Still, the insult of it all was
deeply disturbing. Emily had assumed that *she* would sever her ties
to Vienna when *she* was ready and in the spring of 1953 she had not
yet reached that decision. No doubt Tony played a big part in the
oft-postponed decision to return home.

If Emily gave any thought as to reasons for the decision at
the Secretariat, she might have recalled a seemingly routine
event that occurred more than a year earlier. On March 24,
1952, an investigator from U.S. Army Intelligence interviewed
Emily regarding her past affiliations to organizations deemed un-
American. In fact, the man was not particularly friendly to Emily, as
if trying to trap her into saying something she didn't mean to say.

Back in July of 1951 when Emily applied for her position with
the Four-Power Secretariat, she was asked about "organizations
with which affiliated other than religious or political organizations
or those which show religious or political affiliations." Her written
response: "None at present other than Veterans' Organizations in
America."

From the ample documents that first came to light in 2002*,
it is not clear on what grounds—routine or otherwise—a detailed

---

* Memorandum from the USCOA [Four-Power Commission] Security Branch
dated 27 November 1951.

investigation was ordered. The investigation began quietly with a search of membership lists for a number of domestic organizations labeled "un-American." It seems that at one time or another in the early 1940's, Emily's name had appeared on membership lists of American Youth for Democracy, Minnesota Student League for Democracy, and Young Progressives of America, all termed "subversive" by a committee of the U.S. House Un-American Activities Committee. In March of 1952, the investigation into Emily's past reached directly into the offices of the Four Power Secretariat.

On the 24th of the month, Emily's supervisor was interrogated by an agent of U.S. Army Intelligence. The supervisor described Emily as "a highly diligent employee ...quiet, intelligent, and possesses a definite aptitude for learning languages". The interrogator summarized the supervisor's views.

> *Source believes that SUBJECT studies intensely at the Berlitz School for Languages in Vienna. Source is of the opinion that any person working with the Quadripartite Secretariat would naturally, from the unique experiences gained there, be strongly anti-Communistic. Due to the purely professional relationship of Source with SUBJECT, however, Source does not know SUBJECT's private views on current developments in the world. Source has never heard any information reflecting adversely on SUBJECT.*

Also on the 24th of March the investigating agent interrogated two of Emily's coworkers. They essentially corroborated the supervisor's observations, with additional comments summarized by the investigator in his report:

> *SUBJECT is a very quiet girl, hardworking, extremely studious, serious, and inoffensive. Although she eats almost all of her midday meals in the Quadripartite mess, SUBJECT does not engage, to any noticeable degree, in off-hours discussion, but prefers to utilize this time for language study. ... SUBJECT has never indicated sympathy for any foreign or foreign ideological cause. SUBJECT appears to spend most of her time at work, home, and school, although she does have a boyfriend who also studies at*

Berlitz and with whom SUBJECT is occasionally seen in town. SUBJECT does not mix socially with any of the American girls. … SUBJECT makes an impression of being immature, and does not act as other girls of her age do, perhaps because she is too intellectual. Sources stated they know of no reason to doubt SUBJECT's loyalty and integrity.

To all of this the agent added a note in his report: "Occasional discreet surveillances resulted in observing SUBJECT proceeding either from work to home, or from home to school and return, usually alone and on foot."

On March 25 the agent sought out Emily's friend Tony, who made it quite clear that he was not just an "acquaintance" of Emily, but rather her "friend." According to the agent, Tony "considers her a loyal, intelligent, studious person of sound moral character."

Now it was time to confront the SUBJECT herself. On March 26, the investigating agent arranged to meet Emily privately. He challenged her as to why she had not reported membership in a number of organizations on whose membership list her name was found. Emily did not deny being a member of these various organizations. However, she insisted she was no longer a member and had not been for several years. In his report the agent summarized her responses.

SUBJECT categorized herself as a "liberal" in the 1940's, when she belonged to the listed organizations. She did not believe at the time that these "clubs"operated under Communist direction. But now, after working so closely to the Soviet element in the Quadripartite Secretariat inVienna, she supposes she was "taken in"by the front outfits. The current Communist propaganda, as it emanates openly fromVienna, strikes a familiar chord which SUBJECT formerly heard under the so-called "liberal" titles. SUBJECT stated that she now believes that the Communists direct these front organizations. … SUBJECT stated that because of her "liberal"tendencies, during the 1940's, she was frequently urged to join the Communist Party. Subject answered that she never did join the Communist Party because it was "radical."…

On April 1, 1952, U.S. Army Intelligence submitted its report to the State Department. Surely from Emily's point of view that was the end of it. This confidence would be supported when her annual contract was renewed in July. But in fact, the report from Army Intelligence was only the beginning, for it begot a much deeper investigation.

From detailed FBI memos first released in 2002 it is clear that the FBI was under great pressure. On May 22 a Confidential Memo from J. Edgar Hoover, Director of the FBI, to the field office in Minneapolis: "Conduct a full field Investigation" of Emily Peake, including old files on American Youth For Democracy. The memo demanded a reply by June 23. On August 5, another memo went out to the director of the Minneapolis office, Special Delivery. "This [Emily Peake] loyalty case which is pending in your office is one of the most delinquent loyalty investigations being handled by the Bureau. ... It is your personal responsibility to see that your office meets the deadline in all loyalty cases." A similar memo was delivered to the Minneapolis office a week later. It was not until the middle of September that the Minneapolis office finally submitted its investigative report.

The local office had interrogated ten members of its "informant" pool, none of whom had ever encountered Emily Peake. The one check against her dated back to 1943. While Emily was a part-time student at the University, an FBI informant reported seeing her name on a membership list of American Youth for Democracy, whose president was purported to be a member of the Communist Party. However, in this summer of 1952 the same informant refused to sign any statement to that effect. So much for the informant, but ultimately this would make no difference.

Between June and August of 1952, FBI agents went into the files at Central High School and the University of Minnesota, to Emily's high school friends, to Honeywell, where Emily had worked briefly before and after the war, to Sears Roebuck, where Emily's former boss described her as "hardworking and brilliant," to the Coast Guard, where her performance reviews had been excellent, to co-workers at General Mills, to her Fifth Avenue neighborhood, and to wherever someone might have encountered Emily in her adult life. With every interview the FBI was forced to conclude "there was no question as to [Emily Peake's] loyalty to the United States."

That should have been the end of it. But these were *McCarthy** times, when youthful idealism could end a career for any government employee, especially in the much-maligned State Department. Thus, in July of 1953, Emily Peake was forced to return to the United States. Her relationship with Tony must have ended there, for nothing remains in her well-preserved Vienna papers, not even a picture.

Two years later a treaty between the World War II occupation powers and the Republic of Austria was finally signed. By September, 1955, the 40,000 Soviet troops stationed in Austria had been withdrawn, and by late October the small number of western troops also were gone. The Four-Power Occupation Commission was no more.

---

* In February 1950 U.S. Senator Joseph McCarthy of Wisconsin gave an impassioned speech in which he claimed that the U.S. State Department was riddled with Communists. His words swept the country like wildfire. The senator never did produce the names, but his claims were enough to put the State Department on the defensive.

Return of the Native

Friday Girl

August 1, 1953, was clearly an *epoch*—that moment when a new era commences. In this case, the era was not only *new* in the life journey of Emily Peake, but also *new* in the lives of American Indians throughout the nation.

Let's begin with Emily, who arrived back home in Minneapolis about the first of August. What she found at home was her mother much aged in the three years she was away and Jackie now almost grown, reaching out well beyond the little trio that once was family. Yes, it was good that Emily had come home. The little household certainly demanded not only her presence, but also her undefeated optimism and her energy.

Deep inside, however, Emily was befuddled and angry—why had they fired her in Vienna? Whose fault was it? How dare *they* treat the most loyal of American citizens that way? Had she not served her country in the military and abroad? Had she not stood up for her country whenever it was maligned? Was she not the living example of a downtrodden Indian finding her proper place in the melting pot that *was* America? All of these thoughts stirred in Emily's mind. She had been betrayed by her own government!

It was not in Emily's character to be felled so easily. Years later more than a dozen of her friends and colleagues would utter phrases that rang with similarity: "Emily was never bitter." "She never said a bad word about anybody." "She was happy all the time." "She never

Friday Girl Emily, ca 1956

in her life said an unkind thing about anyone." "She never believed that anyone in the whole world was bad." And on and on.

But for all her idealism and all her infinite faith in human nature, Emily still needed a dependable income. She was now the breadwinner for a family of three—Amie, Adieu,[*] and Jackie. Thus was born FRIDAY GIRL, a creation of the newly entrepreneurial Emily Peake (see Appendix A). FRIDAY GIRL offered "Translations, Secretarial Services and Convention Coverage." And when it came to translations, Emily was not shy. She promised French, German, and Russian. From the scant evidence remaining, she must have delivered accordingly, for FRIDAY GIRL would be in business at least five years.

In those few years, the situation of the Native American community in Minneapolis would change dramatically. Likewise Emily would take on family responsibilities such as she had never imagined. Any dream she might have had of reuniting with Tony, perhaps marrying him, had to be put aside. Dear Tony, to whom she had bid such an unsatisfactory farewell in her hasty departure from Vienna. Like the youthful dream of studying dance, the dream of life with Tony had to be abandoned.

---

[*] Adieu, family name for Emily, derived from her childhood name Abediu.

Relocation/Termination

*Whereas it is the policy of Congress, as rapidly as possible, to make the
Indians within the territorial limits of the United States subject to the
same laws and entitled to the same privileges and responsibilities as
are applicable to other citizens of the United States, to end their status
as wards of the United States, and to grant them all of the rights and
prerogatives pertaining to American citizenship; andWhereas the Indians
within the territorial limits of the United States should assume their full
responsibilities as American citizens. . . .*

—House Concurrent Resolution 108,
August 1, 1953

Until 1953 it was often said that the most devastating blow to the
American Indian, especially to the Ojibwe of Minnesota, was land
allotment—the series of federal laws passed in the late 19th century
that within a single decade stripped the Indian tribes, the bands, and
the people of their land. Whether this outcome was intentional or
an unintended consequence of these laws is of scant importance a
century later. It happened!

World War II intensified the notion of what it was to be
"an American." Not unexpectedly, the definition suggested a
cultural conformity as viewed by the majority population. Native
Americans across the nation had performed admirably during the
war. Approximately 25,000 served in the military, their exploits
often touted—for instance, Ira Hayes of the Pima Tribe, the Indian
Marine who helped raise that first American flag on Iwo Jima; the
Indian radio operators who on the battlefield sent messages that
no enemy had the means to translate, and many others who fought
and sometimes died for America. In addition, another 40,000
Native Americans left their reservations to work in war plants,

133

often moving across the nation. Given an estimated population of 400,000 in 1940, one in six Native Americans—at least one in each family—left the reservation to serve the common good.[17]

There is no record of how many returned to the reservation after the war. Probably most did. Nevertheless, to the majority of the decision makers, the World War II experience proved that Native Americans were ripe for integration. "Set the American Indians free!" was the rallying cry, and by 1953 that cry had reached the floor of the United States Congress.

House Resolution 108 sailed easily through the Senate and was promptly signed by President Dwight Eisenhower. Though the intent of the new law was to be universal, Congress in its wisdom determined to begin slowly.

> Now, therefore, be it Resolved by the House of Representations (the Senate concurring), that it is declared to be the sense of Congress that, at the earliest possible time, all of the Indian tribes and the individual members thereof located within the States of California, Florida, New York, and Texas, and all of the following named Indian tribes and individual members thereof, should be freed from Federal supervision and control and from all disabilities and limitations specially applicable to Indians: the Flathead Tribe of Montana, the Klamath Tribe of Oregon, the Menomonee Tribe of Wisconsin, the Potowatime Tribe of Kansas and Nebraska, and those members of the Chippewa Tribe who are on the Turtle Mountain Reservation, North Dakota. . . .
>
> *House Concurrent Resolution 108 (continued),*
> *August 1, 1953*

One can well imagine the panic that swept across the Ojibwe communities in northern Minnesota. Many White Earth families had roots at Turtle Mountain. Furthermore, historically the Menomonee people were close cousins and still close neighbors to the Ojibwe. So the government would take away what was left of the land—the last vestige of tribal and communal life. For sure White Earth and the other Minnesota Ojibwe reservations were next on the list. Such were the fears that once again brought trauma to each and every Indian community. But the United States government determined to do more, or rather less. That same year, 1953, a subsequent law transferred civil and criminal jurisdiction over what was left of tribal lands in Minnesota and elsewhere to the states. The following year, all of the health programs under the Bureau of Indian Affairs were transferred to the U.S. Public Health Service. Yes, even Big Brother (the BIA)—with whom Native Americans had a century-old love/hate relationship—was about to disappear. So went the lament.

In 1954 the expectation was that the termination of reservations would continue gradually across the nation. Hence, to facilitate integration of these Native inhabitants into urban life, the federal government established three Relocation Centers—Chicago, Cleveland, and Los Angeles. At these centers newcomers would find job training, employment referrals, housing, and other services. The locations were carefully chosen, not only for the availability of unskilled and semiskilled jobs, but also for location. The Relocation Centers must be sufficiently distant from the affected reservations to erase any temptation of "going back." It is sufficient here to say that the relocation effort was mixed at best. Too often it was a disaster for the individuals involved. "Going back" to family, to community, to heritage, was and remains an integral piece of the Native American psyche. This was but one of the many hard lessons learned in the ill-fated relocation/termination years.

Back to the Ojibwe of Minnesota, where the threat of termination hung heavy. Very early it became apparent that few from the Minnesota Ojibwe communities were willing to go as far as Chicago. The Bureau of Indian Affairs relented and began offering services to encourage relocation to Minneapolis. "Every Indian who wanted to go to Minneapolis, Chicago, Cleveland, or Los Angeles received a one-way bus ticket, two weeks in a motel, and two weeks of cheap restaurant food."[18]

Migration to the city, not only from the Ojibwe reservations, but also from the tiny Dakota reservations, now began in earnest. At White Earth the population would fall by fifty percent in the coming decade.

The U.S. Congress's grand scheme for Termination of Indian Reservations never went beyond the initial five: "The Flathead Tribe of Montana, the Klamath Tribe of Oregon, the Menomonee Tribe of Wisconsin, the Potowatime Tribe of Kansas and Nebraska, and those members of the Chippewa Tribe who are on the Turtle Mountain Reservation, North Dakota." If one could identify a single person as the one who stopped the policy dead in its tracks, it was Roger Jourdain, Chairman of the Red Lake Ojibwe Reservation. He was a visionary, a man with immense political clout, an autocrat, fearless and in many cases unforgiving. He served in the tradition of the Red Lake hereditary chiefs, who never ceded their remaining Red Lake lands to the United States and who were never seduced by the promises of individual "allotments." In the mid-20th century Roger Jourdain not only succeeded in resisting "termination," but convinced the leaders of the great western tribes to do the same. So strong did the Native American opposition become that Congress reversed its policy, but not soon enough for the Flatheads, the Klamaths, the Potowatimes, and the Turtle Mountain people. Their reservations were indeed terminated. But the Menomonee Reservation, after a disastrous period under termination, was actually restored to the tribe.

Roger Jourdain died in March of 2002. Native Americans across the land owe more than a little to this steadfast Ojibwe leader.

No Longer Invisible

Responding to the threat of termination, the Indian population in Minneapolis began a spectacular growth, from 426 in 1950 to 3,085 in 1960, a sevenfold increase in a single decade. Probably for the first time ever the Bureau of Indian Affairs took notice of this dramatic development. Historically, the BIA saw its responsibilities only in terms of "trust lands," and those who occupied these lands.

The urban Indian was not part of the BIA responsibility. But times were changing. Responding to intense pressure from the fledgling Indian community and from others, the BIA established an employment office in Minneapolis. The city was actually beginning to take note of these newcomers. One could say that a few churches had always taken note, especially St. Stephens Catholic Church and Gethsemane Episcopal Church. But in 1952, even the Minneapolis Council of Churches established a special Division of Indian Work. Likewise in St. Paul, where the Indian community was smaller and mostly of the Dakota Tribe, the Council of Churches hired a social worker to locate and work with Indian people.*

The decade of the 1950s also turned out to be the wakeup call for Minneapolis's once-invisible Indian community. Already in 1951 several women from Louise Peake's Sah-Kah-Tay Club brought a newspaper reporter into the Art Institute, there to protest the display of a painting depicting a "savage" Indian on horseback. A photo of the event was published in the newspaper and the Institute removed the painting. Even the Broken Arrow Guild now had more visibility. These faithful women, including Louise, still met weekly, bringing along the small children or grandchildren under their care, energetically sewing pajama sets, pedal pushers, blouses, shorts for Indian children, and doing what they loved to do most—designing and creating prize quilts for sale. Twice a year they held a festival, hoping to earn enough to support college scholarships, for in those days neither the state nor federal government was in that business

---

* These U.S. census figures are probably off by at least a factor of two, for in those decades, "Indian" identification was the responsibility of the census-taker, not the individual. According to Indian service organizations, there were in 1960 some 5,000 Indians living in Minneapolis and 2,000 to 3,000 living in St. Paul.[19] The growth of the Native American population in Minneapolis continued through 1990: 5,829 in 1970, 8,933 in 1980, 12,335 in 1990, even as the population of the city fell from a high of 521,718 in 1950 to 368,383 in 1990. The 2000 U.S. census, however, records the Minneapolis Native American population at 8,378, a marked decrease even as the overall Minneapolis population grew slightly to 382,618. Reasons given: A move to the suburbs, not unlike other segments of the population; also the Indian casinos, which have brought a modicum of prosperity to some reservations.

when it came to the urban Indian. But there was never enough money. The best they could do was provide prescription glasses for children in need, plus recipes,* friendship, and mutual support for each other. Over four decades the Broken Arrow Guild would be an icon in the Minneapolis Indian community.

A number of Native American organizations emerged in this decade, some later disappearing, others merging into larger organizations, and a few surviving to this day. The early leadership came directly out of Fred Peake's Twin Cities Chippewa Council. Emily and Louise Peake were the first to remind others of dear Papa's contribution to this urban community. American Indians Incorporated was born in 1950. During the 1950s, it met once a month at the Japanese American Community Center and published a monthly *Peace Pipe*. Another group, the Chippewa Tomahawk Band, sought "to promote the common welfare of the Indian people" by publishing a newsletter entitled *The New Tomahawk*. In St. Paul, the Indian Dance Club emerged in 1959 and a year later renamed itself the St. Paul Indian Club.

All of these organizations, and perhaps others not brought to the attention of this author, looked to a time when a single Indian Center would emerge, not only to provide needed services to the growing Native American community, but more important, to help *forge* such a community that crossed lines of band, tribe, blood-ratio, and economic status. It may not be coincidental that the first discussions of such a center took place in 1954, soon after Emily Peake returned from abroad—quiet meetings in various homes with Emily, James Longie, once of Turtle Mountain, and others who would become Emily's friends and colleagues for life.

---

* Winnie Fairbanks Jourdain, a founder and longtime president of the Broken Arrow Guild, was known for her traditional Wild Rice recipe: "1 cup wild rice, 3 cups rich soup stock of chicken or beef, 1 tsp. vinegar, 1½ tsp. salt. Wash rice thoroughly. Let stand in boiling water for 20 minutes. Drain off water. Place in casserole (with a tight cover). Add soup stock to which vinegar and salt have been added. Cover and bake 1½ hours in a slow oven (300 degrees). For a gourmet touch, add diced chicken and mushrooms. About six servings."[20] In 2001 Winnie died. She was 101 years old, the last survivor of the Broken Arrow Guild.

Spider Woman

According to Navaho legend, eons and eons ago the earth was covered by many floods. Each time the flood came, the Spider Woman lifted the people up to the next level. That was Emily. She pulled people up to a higher level, in understanding, in service and in just plain goodness.
            —Myles Goddard, a mixed-blood Ojibwe

For almost five years FRIDAY GIRL had provided the financial support for Louise, Emily, and Jackie, but it was always a struggle. Emily finally accepted the fact that she couldn't do it all by herself. In 1959 she closed the office and took a position as office secretary in a well-known paint firm, Forman and Ford. She would be with the firm for almost a decade. Now with the luxury of Saturdays free, she was able to return to her earlier love—working with children, all kinds of children—where else but at Waite Neighborhood House on Park Avenue. This was the same magical old mansion where Emily had taught dance a decade earlier, but at that time it was called Elliot Park Neighborhood House. Now with a new name[*] and a new director,[†] Waite House was ripe for the likes of Emily Peake.

Emily promptly organized a Saturday children's program with recreation, neighborhood tours, and just plain being together. Most of the children were from needy families. Many were Native Americans, some were African-Americans, others mixes of every hue, and a few just run-of-the-mill white. To Emily they were all the same, each one special in some unique way. Enter now a young

---

[*] Honoring Edward F. Waite (1860-1958), the Hennepin County Juvenile Court judge who revolutionized the juvenile court system by putting the child's interest above all else.
[†] Archie Goldman, social worker from New York, who recognized the growing presence of Native Americans in the neighborhood and set about to make Waite House responsive to their needs and interests.

man originally from Chicago. His name was Myles Goddard, and back in 1957 he had enrolled at St. Paul Seminary to study for the priesthood. After a year Myles left the seminary but remained in the Twin Cities, teaching at a pre-seminary high school. He had heard about the Ojibwe woman at Waite House, and he wanted to meet her, for Myles was longing to connect with his own Ojibwe roots. One Saturday morning he came by and met the little woman who would change his life. So said Myles many years later. Emily promptly put him in touch with Ojibwe second cousins whom he never knew existed, and she also recruited him for her Saturday morning children's group. Over a period of three years, Emily and Myles led the "Saturday Club" at Waite House. For six weeks every summer they jointly ran the Waite House summer camp at Norway Point on the St. Croix River. According to Myles, a great deal of Emily's Forman and Ford salary was spent on behalf of these Saturday Club children. When Myles was confined to his bed with a blood clot, Emily organized a Saturday bicycle brigade—forty children on bicycles of every size and condition, pedaling out from Minneapolis through the great Theodore Wirth Park system to Myles's home in Golden Valley, each child bearing a homemade gift of one kind or another.

Myles Goddard came to love Emily Peake as a true soul mate. He would have liked to marry her, but he never declared his love beyond that of a devoted nephew toward a doting aunt. He was sixteen years younger than Emily and intellectually he knew marriage was out of the question. In 1963 Myles married someone else and returned to Illinois to teach. Yet he and Emily maintained a close friendship all through the last decades of her life.

Family Matters II

There was a dark side to Emily's life,
a side she would never admit to.
        —Frances Green Anderson, lifelong friend

What Frances referred to as Emily's dark side was the immense family responsibilities she inherited, beginning the day she returned from Europe and continuing almost to the end of her life.

Initially these responsibilities involved niece Jackie, who in 1953 was a rebellious adolescent. Where Emily's mother had worried herself sick over daughter Natalie's teenage escapades, it was now Emily's turn to worry about Natalie's daughter Jackie. But Jackie was of tougher stuff than her frail mother. It was only that she marched to a different drum, one that neither Louise nor Emily could fully understand.

In 1957 Jackie married one Leonard Mims and moved to North Minneapolis. Time for Louise and Emily to downsize. After more than thirty years on Fifth Avenue, Emily gave up the flat and leased a one-bedroom apartment in a fourplex at 1925 Second Avenue South, the heart of the Stevens Square neighborhood. This was a modest neighborhood, historically a first stop for newcomers who moved in and later moved on. In the 1950s the newcomers were mostly Native Americans. Some moved on into the mainstream; others moved back to the reservation; and some stayed.* Emily would live in Stevens Square the rest of her life.

But back to the newlyweds, Jackie and Leonard Mims. Leonard was black—African-American, as we say today. Out of this marriage were born two daughters, Evon in 1958 and Suzan in 1960. In some

---

* In the 1960s the newcomers tended to be African-Americans from Chicago and elsewhere; in the 1970s and 1980s many newcomers were from Southeast Asia, especially Vietnam and Cambodia. The 1990s brought refugees from Somalia and Ethiopia. Always Stevens Square is changing, yet in some ways always the same.

ways, Jackie Mims was her mother's daughter, for she and Leonard were committed to the Socialist Workers' Party. They were known as Trotskyites, for they remained loyal to Leon Trotsky, an early leader of the Russian Revolution who had fled to Mexico when Josef Stalin took over. In 1940 Trotsky was assassinated, by order of Stalin himself. Since Jackie and Leonard were openly committed to the Socialist cause, even though anti-Stalinist, their names soon

Emily's family: Suzy, Jackie, Evon, Adieu (Emily), and Amie (Louise), 1966

appeared on an FBI list. The Mimses decided to leave the country, go to Fidel Castro's new Cuba, a place where their kind would be respected. Thus, in 1961, when Suzie was just six months old, the little family of four flew down to Cuba. At the time the country was absolutely impoverished. On their arrival Jackie and Leonard discovered that support for the Revolution was not enough. They were viewed as just four more mouths to feed. Come back later when things are better! So did the Cubans advise them.

Leonard and Jackie returned to Minneapolis and to the jobs they had left behind. Not unexpectedly, they were now hounded by the

FBI. Federal agents were asking questions of their coworkers as well as their employers. In the midst of this heightened trauma, Leonard began acting strange. In fact, his behavior was such that mental health authorities intervened. Leonard Mims was committed to St. Peter Hospital, where a brain tumor was diagnosed. It would eventually cause his death. Time for Jackie to go her own way, this time with a young man, John Heine. One day Jackie dropped Evon and Suzie off with Amie and Emily and promptly left for California. Evon and Suzie would spend the rest of their childhood with Emily.

Louise Peake—Amie to all those who loved her—died in the spring of 1967. The funeral service in Minneapolis was well attended, for over the years much of the Indian community had come under Amie's care in one way or another. She who had been baptized and confirmed in the Catholic Church died an Episcopalian. Thus, after the service, Emily and Jackie accompanied Louise's remains to White Earth for burial in the St. Columba Episcopal cemetery—St. Columba, out of Father En-megah-bowh's early mission, where Emily's paternal grandmother, Keche-ogemah—later, Grandma Schneider—had her first school lessons. Yet Grandma Schneider, who was baptized and confirmed in the Episcopal Church by none other than Bishop Whipple, as an adult had left the church. She died a Catholic and is buried at White Earth in St. Anne's Catholic Church cemetery.

Of what importance is all this? Ever since the first Christian missionaries arrived, the tug between two great churches—Catholic and Episcopal—has been an ongoing event in Ojibwe history. In every generation, individuals and families turn from one to the other, for reasons much less profound than their respective theologies. Even to this day, when these two great branches of Christianity move closer to each other, the political dynamics at White Earth have more than a little to do with church affiliation.

In Minneapolis, Emily connected Evon and Suzie to Gethsemane Episcopal Church, where she had been confirmed. Emily attended every PTA meeting at Madison School, and increasingly spoke out that the Minneapolis Public Schools were woefully neglectful when it came to inner city children. Evon and Suzie learned early to run errands and to shop for busy Adieu. Even to this day they are remembered as frequent visitors to the corner grocery, "the dear little Peake girls who so clung to their auntie."[21]

In these years Emily was moving far beyond race and ethnic origin when it came to her unwavering defense of children. In her later public life, when others marveled at her fierce commitment to children of every color and origin, Emily would reply, "I owe it all to Evon and Suzie."

Emily had never used her Veteran's housing benefit, namely, a low-interest mortgage to buy a home. When the house next to the fourplex came on the market, it was time for Emily to act. In 1970 she bought the little house and moved in with her two grandnieces. Certainly the house was not much to look at, but it had two bedrooms and a small room in back, which Emily promptly claimed as her office. Oh how proud she was of the little office and the bit of privacy it provided. 1919 Second Avenue would be home to Emily for the rest of her life. Not only Evon and Suzie grew up there. A decade later Jackie's three Heine sons would also call 1919 home. Emily's place became a drop-in center for her friends and a meeting place whenever a new idea was percolating in the community. Like the Peake flat a generation earlier, from which Louise Peake never turned anyone away, so it was in Emily's time at 1919 Second Avenue.

In 1974 Suzie gave birth to a son, David. Still too young to take on motherly duties, she promptly turned the infant over to Emily. She would adopt the boy, give him her family name "Peake" and raise him almost to adulthood. Emily would be every bit as devoted to David as she was to his mother, to his Auntie Evon, and to his grandmother Jackie.

How Emily, working full time and deeply involved in Indian and civic issues, ever managed we shall never know. Some of her greatest public achievements occurred precisely in these years. Yet in the last decade of her life, a devoted friend, Hy Rosen, concluded that Emily had always wished for a husband, at least for someone who might have shared her family responsibilities.

Birth of an Indian Center

Among the many organizations in which Emily Peake had leadership roles, the one that bears her deepest handprint is the Upper Midwest American Indian Center. Its beginnings go back to the 1950s and an informal group of Indian people from Minneapolis—both Ojibwe and Dakota. They met and they dreamed and they formed the outline of a center *by* Indian people and *for* Indian people. One evening in 1961 the decision was made—they* would put the vision on paper, incorporate, and bring it all to life.

On June 9, 1961, the Articles of Incorporation† were signed and sealed. The Upper Midwest American Indian Center was no longer just a dream. It had arrived. For the next five years, this Indian Center would be run totally by volunteers. Its location depended on the generosity of like-minded people and institutions—initially a bit of space downtown in the offices of the Twin Cities Chippewa Tribal Council. Even without funds the fledgling center grew.

It sponsored monthly powwows, a sewing class, a drum club, and children's programs, all in donated space at Waite House. It was the powwows, however, that truly brought the Upper Midwest Indian Center to life. And as it has always been with church suppers, so was it with these powwows. The women were in charge—Emily Peake, Winnie Jourdain, Rose Bluestone, and Jessie Larson—making the rules (no alcohol), bringing something for the potluck and encouraging others to do the same, generally orchestrating the entire evening. Emily's duties went beyond that. She wanted the world to know that the Ojibwe and the Dakota of Minneapolis were together building a community in this otherwise foreign land.

---

* Present at the meeting were Eddie Benton, Fred Blessing, Rose Bluestone, Dan Hardy, Frank and Louise Hurd, Jim Longie, George Mitchell, and Emily Peake, a mix of tribal connections.

† See Appendix B.

The world did take notice, especially the Catholic and Episcopal churches. Time to invite the bishops of both churches to an Indian Center powwow. Both accepted.*

That evening the drummer sat ready with his drum, a goodly number of participants were wearing their ceremonial dress, and the space nearly trembled with high anticipation. Suddenly a group of some fifteen Ojibwe young people burst in the door, all of them quite inebriated. What to do? Jessie, the Dakota Elder, allowed that the intruders must be thrown out before the bishops arrived. Emily had a better way. "Start the drum," she ordered. "This first dance a snake dance." With young Myles Goddard in the lead and Jessie Larson close behind, followed by Rose and Winnie and Emily, the others were quick to join in. Thus the dance began. What a surprise it must have been—around the room, through the Waite House front door, outside into the fifteen-degree night, around to the side door, back to the powwow room, once more out of the building, around to the side and back in, round and round, always the drum to keep up the fervor. After four excursions, the snake dance ended. The inebriates? Indeed, they had become quite sober. By the time the two bishops arrived, all was in order. Emily called for the honor dance—that most special form of the round dance—with the two bishops in the lead, each flanked on one side by an Ojibwe and on the other by a Dakota. That night Emily Peake had succeeded in turning disaster into triumph. It wasn't the first time and it wouldn't be the last.

Archie Goldman, Waite House director, was very generous when it came to Indian-sponsored activities, for they fit well with the Waite House Indian bent. Thus, even without a home of its own, the unfunded Upper Midwest center flourished and attracted ever more attention. It had become a beacon for the Native Americans and a cause celebré for local do-gooders. In 1967 Mayor Arthur Naftalin created the Minneapolis Committee on American Indian Affairs and attached it to the new Minneapolis Commission on Human Rights. The mayor appointed ten Native Americans

---

* Catholic Bishop Leonard Cowley and Episcopal Bishop Philip McNairy.

to the Committee, each representing a group within the Indian community. He made Emily Peake of the Chippewa Tribal Council chairman. How effective was the Committee? At this late date it is difficult to say. The late 1960s were times of radical change in Minneapolis and elsewhere. These were times of militancy on many fronts, including a new generation of urban Indian people.

In 1964 President Lyndon Johnson had announced his War on Poverty and persuaded the U.S. Congress to create an Office of Economic Opportunity to fund hundreds, if not thousands, of grass roots organizations across the nation. The War on Poverty was designed as one grand effort to eliminate poverty everywhere. In 1966 the Upper Midwest American Indian Center received a major grant under this program, enough money to rent suitable space in an abandoned nursery school on the north side of Minneapolis, enough money to have a telephone and other office supplies, and best of all, enough money to hire a full-time director. One Gordon Kendall was the first director. Emily Peake was on the board and for a brief time served as interim director. She also organized the children's programs, which were wont to enter the realm of make-believe. Even the publicity for summer programs had a childlike quality that Emily alone could bring about (see Appendix C).

For Emily, these must have been heady times. She now had a paying appointment teaching American Indian history in the Minneapolis Public Schools and was able to give up her Forman and Ford secretarial position. From the beginning of the Upper Midwest Center, she had visualized this one institution as the integrating factor for everything needed to build and sustain the urban Indian community, *her* community. She believed that this achievement was close to fruition, having evolved from working together and sometimes compromising, especially when it came to the non-Indian power structure. She saw the Center as proof of the right path to "Red Power," the new word of the late sixties. Emily, however, would be in for a surprise.

Federal funding for the Upper Midwest Indian Center was controlled by a local organization with the benign name of Citizens

Community Centers, Inc. (CCC). The Indian Center was one of three community organizations receiving federal funds through the CCC. Stipulations as to who was eligible to serve on the board and who was eligible to be staff were federally dictated and further interpreted by the local CCC. In May of 1968, the CCC withdrew funding of the Upper Midwest Center, claiming that the board was not militant enough, hence not representative of the targeted "poor" in the city. The staff was dismissed and the rented space abandoned. It appeared that the Upper Midwest American Indian Center was dead.

Red Power

The Great Divide

In the late 1960s hardly a single corner of America was spared from the turmoil that swept across the nation. On the far shores of the Pacific Ocean, American troops were battling an army of well-equipped guerrilla fighters in the deadly jungles of South Vietnam. This army was known as the Viet Cong. Communist revolutionaries, we called them, for they were backed and supplied by the Communist government of North Vietnam. It was a war that the United States had slipped into almost unwittingly. The first involvement was innocent enough. In 1961 the United States provided military advisors to the government of South Vietnam in its efforts to quell a revolution. Three years later an attack on a United States destroyer propelled the nation into its first combat role. Within a few months thousands of American troops were on the ground and in the air on an Asian peninsula far, far from home. The year 1965 saw the beginning of an antiwar sentiment that would sweep across the United States, a sentiment severely impacting the morale of the troops fighting in Vietnam and seriously damaging the effectiveness of the president, Lyndon Johnson. The antiwar rage would escalate to the point of direct interference with the nation's domestic tranquility—violent confrontations between protesters and police at the 1968 National Democratic Convention, antiwar demonstrations nationwide culminating in a Washington, D.C., demonstration that involved 250,000 protesters. After the killing of four Kent State students by National Guard troops in a demonstration that went amuck, college campuses were in such an uproar that at least one hundred colleges were closed. That year, 1970, a draft lottery was activated, a lottery that generally exempted students enrolled in higher education. America had become a nation divided against itself. It would be another three years before a new president, Richard Nixon, would gradually extricate America from Vietnam. In 1975 South Vietnam would fall and Vietnam would be reunited under the Communists.

But in 1970, protest and militancy were the bywords—not only against the war, but also against a multitude of injustices, both real and perceived. It was common knowledge that both Blacks and Native Americans were statistically over-represented when it came to those fighting and dying in the jungles of Vietnam. This tilt was even more obvious once the military draft lottery took hold. A bitterness quite apart from antiwar sentiment, in fact, a counterforce to antiwar sentiment, gripped large elements of the minority communities.

Which brings us back to Minneapolis and East Franklin Avenue, an area increasingly populated by Native Americans. In fact, local pundits called the neighborhood "the Reservation," a term the Indian people resented. The Minneapolis police, as much through ignorance as due to ill will, were inclined to treat this population with disrespect, if not disdain. But now a new element entered the picture. Native American Vietnam veterans, having served their stint, were trickling back to Minnesota, a number of them settling along East Franklin Avenue. Like other veterans of that conflict, they were stunned by the public contempt for their military involvement. Add to this the desperate state of many of their Native American brethren, these Indian veterans determined to take matters into their own hands. The spark that ignited their militancy occurred one warm summer evening. Though some of the details have been lost in the retelling, the drama evolved more or less as follows: A call to the police that some eight drunk Indians were disturbing the peace, generally being a nuisance along the avenue. The police arrived in a van that could only hold four prisoners. What to do about the other four in order to hold them until the van returned for a second load? The police had a solution. Handcuff the four drunks together to a light post until the officers returned after delivering the first load to jail. And so it was done.

Out of that night was born the Indian Patrol—Vietnam veterans and other Native Americans intent on confronting and challenging whoever was to blame when it came to their own people. The rest of that summer, the Indian Patrol was a benevolent presence in the Franklin Avenue neighborhood, watching and reporting on the police and any other authority they deemed guilty of disrespect or worse. Out of the Indian Patrol was born the American Indian Movement.* Almost like a wildfire, AIM spread across state and tribal borders to become a national movement, occasionally violent, generally not, but always confrontational, initiating encounters that have changed the national and international landscape.

---

* Although in recent decades AIM's activities on the national level have made the most news, AIM's record of successes in Minnesota is no less than astounding. Early on, AIM took control of the church-sponsored Division of Indian Work; initiated the Minneapolis Indian Health Board and the Legal Rights Center; occupied the Naval air station to demand grants for Indian education; assisted the Lac Courte Orieles Ojibwe of Wisconsin in the takeover of a dam that would have flooded 25,000 acres of tribal land; founded two Indian-based schools, one a public school in Minneapolis, the other a charter school in St. Paul; sponsored the Indian-run Little Earth housing project in Minneapolis; introduced in the Minnesota Legislature American Indian language and culture legislation that is now a model across the nation; established the first education program for American Indian offenders at the Minnesota State Prison; founded the Circle of Life Survival School on the White Earth Reservation; established the American Indian Opportunities Industrialization Center in Minneapolis; created the Anishinabe Akeeng Organization to regain tax-forfeited and otherwise lost land on the White Earth Reservation; restarted the AIM Patrol in Minneapolis to deal with serial killings of American Indian women; founded the Elaine M. Stately Indian Youth Services to divert Indian youth from gang involvement; established the Peacemaker Center in Minneapolis; created the Sacred Pipe Sundance festival at the Minnesota pipestone quarries, an annual gathering of Ojibwe Nations and Dakota communities; at the 1992 Super Bowl, led a massive protest against Indian names for sports teams; worked successfully with the students of Macalaster College in St. Paul to cancel the commencement address of Ted Turner, owner of the Atlanta *Braves*, a name considered demeaning to the Indian people.[22]

The Minneapolis American Indian Center

Emily really designed the Center. I was just the draftsman.
—Thomas Hodne, Architect[23]

In the midst of continuing turmoil in the nation, in Minneapolis, and along Franklin Avenue, Emily Peake and her staff from the presumably defunct Upper Midwest Center moved into leased office space at 817 East Franklin. A new Minneapolis American Indian Center, this one funded by the CCC, was about to be born. Emily took as her most urgent task to bring about the design, the funding, and the building of this new American Indian Center. Architecturally it should represent the expectations of the increasingly militant Native American community. One can imagine Emily viewing this as the opportunity for which she had been preparing all her life. (She was forty-eight years old in 1968.) One day she knocked on the door of Hodne and Stageberg Architects. Their offices were just a few blocks away in one of Minneapolis's grand old stone mansions. As Tom Hodne remembers it, the woman seemed to be in a hurry. She told the secretary she wanted to see the architect who was designing a housing complex in East Harlem, New York. When the secretary suggested making an appointment with Mr. Hodne, the woman became a bit feisty. "Time is of the essence," said she. Tom left his design table to see what the ruckus was all about and in this way first met Emily Peake. He promptly became her partner in design. Their personal friendship would become lifelong.

Decades later, Architect Hodne marvels at Emily's creativity along with her good sense. Together she and the architect looked over various sites. They settled on the site of an abandoned elementary school at 1530 East Franklin. The property was owned by the city. Should they remodel the old school? Emily was adamant; the answer was no! And what about design? The building must face Franklin Avenue, for this avenue was the focus of the Indian community. How to fulfill the spiritual needs of this community? Even here Emily's voice was the strong one—within the building a large circle, a sacred circle at the heart of the community, with a seating area all around. Outside the building a smaller circle, where the children could play. Emily was in the design loop from

The Minneapolis American Indian Center,
1530 East Franklin Avenue, 1975
MHS photo by Steve Plattner

beginning to end. Even in small details, Hodne and his associates made changes based on Emily's advice. With her input, the design seemed to take on a life of its own.

But there were other considerations, mainly funding. Thanks to Hubert Humphrey, who never missed a beat even after he was defeated for United States president, federal money for the project was promptly forthcoming. Before it was all over, the city and state would also do their part. The city gave the land but retained ownership, agreeing to be responsible for outside maintenance until some undetermined future time.* In 1974 groundbreaking took place, and on May 5, 1975, the Minneapolis American Indian Center† was dedicated. Emily Peake was not invited to participate in either event. As far as we know, she was not even present.

The modern American Indian Center became Tom Hodne's springboard as preferred architect for the design of twenty-seven Native American projects. Of these, twenty-three have been built, including and especially the Tribal College building at Cloquet, Minnesota. Tom maintains that he owes it all to Emily, not only the opportunities, but also the concept of "dual culture," which Emily was more inclined to term "culture bridges."

But back to 1969, when the Indian Center design was well under way. In January Matthew Eubanks became director of CCC, Inc. Experienced in the militant black movement, he set about to create an environment more in keeping with AIM's philosophy of confrontation. At the monthly meetings of the Indian Center advisory council, Tom Hodne regularly updated the council on design progress. He soon became aware that Emily had little role in the decision-making process. She was never called upon to contribute, nor did she volunteer information. Yet she was the director! Was the council aware of Emily's deep involvement in the design process? Apparently not. Tom determined it was not his place to ask such questions. In August it would all become clear to him, and to the public.

In August, at a special meeting of the Minneapolis American Indian Center advisory council, twenty-four of the thirty present voted to have Emily Peake removed as director. Emily was not present at the meeting. The reasons given were somewhat spurious, mainly that "Miss Peake could not communicate with many of the

---

* Over the years this arrangement has caused problems, the Center claiming that the city has seriously nreglected its commitment. At the writing of this tale, discussions are underway to find a better solution for both the city and the center.
† At the dedication, the center carried the name "Minneapolis Regional Native American Center." In 1980 it was renamed "Minneapolis American Indian Center."

Indian youth and members of the American Indian Movement [AIM]." For Emily this must have been a bitter moment. Yet by the next day she had a prepared statement for the press.

> *The black militants are in control of the CCCs. They have aided the American Indian Movement in their intent to take over the American Indian CCC. Matthew Eubanks has allowed AIM members to infiltrate and finally control the citizens' advisory council of the Indian Center. . . . The meeting [last night] was packed by AIM members and by teen-agers brought from the American Indian Teen Center. . . . The Indian community is beginning to pull together. Attacks by AIM members on other Indians have helped to unite them.* [24]

Within a few days, Emily had gathered colleagues from several Indian groups, including board members of the reborn but struggling Upper Midwest American Indian Center. They too would go after federal funding, but not through CCC. The Upper Midwest would proceed under the auspices of the Hennepin County antipoverty programs and prepare a proposal directly to the federal Mobilization of Economic Resources office. There was no reason a city the size of Minneapolis couldn't have two Indian centers. According to Emily, they would have Minneapolis's new mayor Charles Stenvig as well as Minnesota's Senator Walter Mondale on their side.

Not One, But Two American Indian Centers

The Upper Midwest American Indian Center, stripped of its CCC funding source in the spring of 1968, had nevertheless refused to die. Most of the board members had been involved from the beginning, a mix of committed Indian and non-Indian activists, all sharing a common vision of what an Indian Center ought to be. Nevermind that the CCC was building an Indian Center on Franklin Avenue. The CCC-supported protagonists were the latecomers while the Upper Midwest Center was here to stay! So must have been the view of the board, for in the course of one year, the Upper Midwest Center successfully obtained an interim funding commitment from the United Way with the promise of more. Thus, in May of 1969, the Center hired Bob Carr, a Pueblo, as director, and Joyce Yellowhammer, an Ojibwe and former staff member, as secretary. After moving in and out of temporary offices, the newly funded Upper Midwest Center settled into tiny rented quarters in South Minneapolis, less than two miles from the proposed new Minneapolis American Indian Center on East Franklin.

The CCC-sponsored Indian Center did not take lightly to this rebirth of a potential competitor, and certainly not to its United Fund support. Without the Upper Midwest Center these funds might well have been designated for programs at the Franklin Avenue Indian Center. The stage was now set for a serious confrontation. The place: the Minnesota Urban Indian Federation.

At the request of AIM's Clyde Bellecourt, the chairman of the Federation called a special meeting on May 21. At this meeting, Clyde submitted a motion that the Federation ask the Health and Welfare Council (conduit for United Fund support) to reconsider and redirect United Way funding from Upper Midwest American Indian Center to the Minneapolis American Indian Center. His motion was voted down eight to one.

Which brings us to the genius of Clyde Bellecourt, founder and longtime president of AIM, more recently founder and president of the Peacemakers Center. Clyde's roots, like Emily's, go back to the Crane clan, the orators of the tribe. Like Emily, Clyde is a descendant of the Mississippi band of Ojibwe, and like Emily in her way, Clyde has a personality that says "follow me." The differences between these two individuals are mighty, so mighty as to mask their similarities. Emily avoided confrontation. She used persuasion and compromise to work around it, but she nevertheless remained directed toward her ultimate goal. Emily Peake rarely gave up. On the other hand, Clyde Bellecourt believed, and still believes, in confrontation. His entire career has validated this means to an end. But Clyde also has a brilliant grasp of the realm of the possible. At that May 21 meeting, the long-brewing confrontation of two fledgling urban American Indian community centers had indeed come to a head. The Federation was being forced to choose between two centers, each supported by a substantial number of committed Native Americans. Clyde must have understood what was happening before his very eyes—the fragmentation of the American Indian community, which more than a few non-Indians would have liked to see happen.

To the astonishment of those gathered, Clyde Bellecourt submitted a second motion—that the Urban Indian Federation continue to work with the Minneapolis American Indian Center and that the Upper Midwest American Indian group continue to work on its center with the hope that eventually the two would come together. This motion passed by a vote of twelve to one.

Thirty-four years later the Upper Midwest American Indian Center and the Minneapolis American Indian Center are still two distinct organizations.

Emily in Charge I

Indians are independent thinkers. We all have different
ways of doing things and thinking about things.
—Emily Peake, 1970[25]

The decade of the 1970s was perhaps the most verdant of the century when it came to new optimism, energy, and ideas within the Indian community, not to mention the possibility of funding more than a few of these. The Upper Midwest American Indian Center now acquired a place of its own at 1113 West Broadway. Nevermind that a mortgage came with it. Emily's friend Hy Rosen had arranged it all. He even found tenants for the street-front portion of the building—Pilot City, a federally funded effort to build community on the city's near north side.* Within a month of Emily's removal from the CCC-sponsored Franklin Avenue Indian Center, she was already on the staff of the reborn Upper Midwest Center. Emily would say that her heart had always been there. As a new paid employee responsible for finding housing and employment for newcomers, Emily was a whiz. Her contacts went far beyond the Indian community. She knew everyone, and she used them all. It would later be said that tiny Emily Peake was the "biggest beggar" around. For those in need, she was always a friend. She could find Christmas turkeys, Easter hams, emergency groceries, housing, and a first job. Besides, Emily's home was the twenty-four-hour drop-in center, and drop in they did, especially after she moved to her little house at 1919 Second Avenue South.

Mayor Charles Stenvig was an early supporter of "Emily's way." In January of 1970, he appointed her to the Minneapolis Human Rights Commission, which prompted the *Minneapolis Star* to do a major article on her philosophy as well as her accomplishments. It seems appropriate that the accompanying photo showed Emily reading a book, *Indians in America,* to Evon and Suzie—Jackie's daughters—who had been with Emily almost since infancy. Emily's appointment to the Human Rights Commission was the mayor's signal that this agency should be more representative of the urban population. Oddly enough, even this appointment was

---

*Hy Rosen, a product of Minneapolis's north side: For close to eighty years, North Minneapolis had been home to immigrants and their descendents from Central Europe, including a large number of Jews. Theirs was a strong neighborhood with a lively business component spread out along Plymouth Avenue. Among the many Plymouth Avenue grocery stores was Hy's Dairy. His home stood a few houses down on the same street. After World War II the neighborhood changed. New immigrants arrived, from places like Chicago and points south. These new immigrants were generally Blacks, more likely than not also poor and without jobs. Gradually the Jewish population moved to the suburbs, but still the businesses remained. Then over one hot summer week in 1966, following the Los Angeles Watts race riots, "they" destroyed Plymouth Avenue, all the Jewish businesses and more. As Hy Rosen later described it, "I stood behind the counter with a butcher

controversial. Emily replaced Commissioner Raymond Plank, a leading citizen from Wayzata. He objected to several of Stenvig's appointments, claiming these urban appointees would have no clout in the community.

About this time also, Emily was appointed to the Minnesota Indian Affairs Commission, her role to represent the urban Indian community. Also on the commission was Vernell Wabasha, director the Division of Indian Work in Minneapolis. She represented the combined Minnesota Dakota communities. Thus was born a collegial relationship that would have a mighty impact in the state. "Education" was the reigning word on the Commission—education of the wider community regarding the history of the Indian people, a long neglected—and worse—often distorted history. Where to begin? Why not with the "Sioux Uprising" and the hanging of the thirty-eight Dakota Indians? The name of this so-called war alone had rankled generations of the Dakota. Very likely the renaming of the tragic events—now known as the U.S.-Dakota Conflict—had its origins on the Indian Affairs Commission, where Emily and Vernell stood as one. But that was not enough for these two women. They considered the hangings a dastardly deed, and they wanted this to be a piece of the broader education effort.

Why not a march? Together they sought out Dakota leaders, especially those whose ancestors had been directly involved. It was not difficult, for remnants of the original Dakota bands resided on

---

knife in hand and my wife and children behind me. I knew the black youth in the neighborhood. These were not they. I could see the license numbers on the autos, from out of state. Those fellows came from elsewhere and riled up the local young people, gave them drugs, and told them to go to it." Thus was destroyed what remained of a once solid community in North Minneapolis. The Jews had fled. After Hy's store was destroyed, he too took his family to the suburbs, but Hy never really left. Even before the dust had settled, he became involved with Pilot City, a new federally funded project to stabilize the neighborhood through community building. Hy eventually went on the board of Pilot City. He arranged for the Pilot City $1.00 purchase of a synagogue abandoned by its congregation in the flight to the suburbs. From 1966 to the present, Hy Rosen's well-honed business skills have been directed to the betterment of the human condition in Minneapolis and beyond.

scraps of land returned years earlier by the United States government. Working together, Emily, Vernell, and the handful of Dakota leaders scheduled a march to the site of the Mankato executions. The date: December 26, 1971, anniversary day of the 1862 event. It wouldn't be an easy task. For more than a century no Dakota had deigned to set foot in Mankato, even though several Dakota communities lay nearby. So strong was the lingering bitterness.

Yet the little march went forward. The high temperature that day, fifteen degrees Fahrenheit. The initial gathering place was a Happy Chef Restaurant on Highway 69 out of town. Forty Indian Dakota showed up, most of them descendents of the men who had been executed or imprisoned. They were joined by twenty others. The little group walked the mile and a half to a local Presbyterian church for a lunch of traditional Indian food and an impromptu discussion regarding the original marker of the hanging site—a tall granite stone monument that was now in storage. Carved into the monument in large letters were the words "HERE WERE HANGED 38 SIOUX INDIANS." Underneath in smaller letters, "DEC. 26, 1862." The issue was whether it should be re-installed to mark the site near the Minnesota River. Emily spoke first. "It's a disgraceful thing. We don't want it back there." Another concurred. "Break it into four pieces and drop it in the river." Harold Crooks of Prior Lake, however, disagreed: "I'd like to see it stay there (at the site). People should remember it's a bad thing, but removing it will not erase the evil of the execution. People must remember what happened there." Lack of consensus notwithstanding, the little group left the church and continued the walk to an asphalt-covered apron at the local Standard Oil Station. There once stood the great scaffold and later the disputed monument. It was an extraordinary moment. Norman Blue of Granite Falls read aloud the names of the thirty-eight "who sacrificed their lives for the Dakota people." This was perhaps the first time in history that the thirty-eight had been acknowledged aloud *by name* (see Appendix D). Amos Owen of Prairie Island concluded the ceremony with a prayer in the Dakota language. A day later the Mankato march made front-page news in Minneapolis.[26]

From time to time it happens that a rather obscure event changes the course of history. The Mankato march on a cold December day in 1971 was just that. Thirty years later, a Reconciliation Park and a Reconciliation parkway lie opposite the original execution site. On the spot itself, carved from Minnesota granite, stands a nine-foot-tall stone buffalo, symbol of the Dakota nation. Since 1972 annual powwows and heritage days remind an entire region not only of a terrible time, but also of ongoing reconciliation. And besides, for both Emily and Vernell, this march confirmed that the Ojibwe and the Dakota were indeed brothers and sisters at heart.

Emily was now also vice president of the Upper Midwest Center; board member of STAIRS,* a tutoring program in the public schools; and member of both the Urban Indian Federation and the Minnesota State Educational Committee. What pleased her most of all was the fact that she was vice president of the Twin City Chippewa Tribal Council, founded almost fifty years earlier by her long-deceased Papa. How she managed it all is a mystery. As a matter of fact, she didn't quite. After missing more than three monthly meetings of the Minneapolis Human Rights Commission in a single year, she was dropped from the Commission as required by city code. Still, Mayor Stenvig believed in Emily, and in his mind Emily always delivered. Thus, in 1972, he appointed her to a five-year term on the Minneapolis Housing and Redevelopment Authority, an agency with immense power when it came to public and public/private development. Emily was the first Indian and the first woman to serve on the Commission.

That year Emily was also hired as full-time executive director of the Upper Midwest American Indian Center, which she co-founded a decade earlier. By 1972 this center was a Model Urban Indian Center, one of four in the nation. Later that year, Emily received the highest number of votes in the election of eleven members to the financially powerful Urban American Indian Center, a conduit organized for the funding of other programs. This election again pitted the Upper Midwest Center (UMAIC) against the Minneapolis

---

* STAIRS: Service to American Indian Resident Students.

Indian Center (MAIC). Nine of the eleven members elected were UMAIC-endorsed candidates. Always federal funding and federal stipulations were the issues. The Upper Midwest Center was responsible for distributing federal funds to AIM-sponsored Indian schools in Minneapolis, St. Paul, and Milwaukee. With ill feelings rampant on both sides, it was difficult to get a proper accounting of the federal dollars. Thus, when Emily's Upper Midwest Center was threatened with a federal investigation, she and the board chose to no longer manage these funds. Still, these controversies did nothing to stifle the center's expanding programs. Under Emily's leadership, the Center boasted an Indian Guest House, programs for youth, for senior citizens, for health, housing, job development and employment, Indian school referral, symposiums for non-Indians, a college fund, summer camp, and more.

Indian Fighter

In 1972 neither Minneapolis nor the Upper Midwest Center could avoid the momentous events occurring elsewhere in the nation. That year the American Indian Movement (AIM) led a march on Washington to air grievances accumulated over many years, especially those related to the Bureau of Indian Affairs (BIA). The climax of the march was the occupation of the BIA offices, an event that President Richard Nixon chose not to ignore. Realist that he was, the president consented to meet with AIM representatives and receive from them a list of twenty "solutions" to the nation's sad history of broken treaties. That might have been the end of it, but it was not.

A new and deadlier confrontation was already in the making at Wounded Knee Creek in South Dakota. Back in 1890, a kind of reawakening had occurred among the plains tribes. It was called the Ghost Dance—songs and ceremonies that prophesied a return to life as it had once been before the Europeans arrived.

The United States government, for whatever reason, saw danger in the development and sent troops to quell it. On December 15, the troops killed Sitting Bull, perhaps the greatest Dakota leader ever. Two weeks later the troops killed an entire gathering of 300 unarmed men, women, and children. The event has never been forgotten, nor forgiven. Early in 1973 a group of Dakota, in concert with AIM, gathered at Wounded Knee to demonstrate their claims against the government, especially the broken treaties. It generated a confrontation with less radical elements of the Native community. The demonstrators took over the Pine Ridge trading post and the Catholic church. The tribal government called in the federal government—armed FBI agents—to diffuse the confrontation, but it all turned out otherwise. The occupation lasted seventy-one days; two demonstrators and two FBI agents were killed.

Across the nation, American Indians were moved one way or the other by the drama. In Minneapolis some sixty teenage youths occupied the premises of the Upper Midwest Center. For a number of days they sat, ate, played cards, but otherwise did not destroy any property. At night, twenty or more settled down in sleeping bags and blankets. Their complaint? The Center was neglectful when it came to serving the Native American youth. Their demand? Initially, that a youth representative be appointed to the board and that one-fourth of the Center's budget be directed to youth programs. The program director offered a rather weak response, namely, that they were working on all of this. In the meantime, the entire staff moved its office to the Peake home on Second Avenue. Apparently this enraged the young people even more, for their final demand was that the program director, the executive director—Emily Peake—and the entire board be dismissed for disregarding community involvement. It didn't happen.

While the point was certainly made, another group calling itself Concerned Indian Citizens made its own statement, namely, that the youths did not speak for all Indian youths. And Emily? She decided to fight back. If they would use the press, so would she. Even as the Wounded Knee standoff continued, Emily wrote a letter to the editor of the *Minneapolis Tribune:*

How is it possible that a relatively small group of militant Indians can create such a furor across the countryside not once, but time and time again—Cass Lake, Washington, Custer, Wounded Knee and possibly other points west? How is it this group can be taken seriously when it declares itself to be a sovereign and independent nation ready to do business with the United Nations? How can it destroy government property and not be punished, but instead be given a large amount of money (approximately $67,000) with which to depart?

These are some of the questions being asked by all people, Indian and non-Indian alike. Who has created these great heroes for the Indian community? Certainly not the Indians. As usual, nobody has bothered to consult them.

This is a time when the press and other media can have a good show, especially since the Indians are looking and acting the way they should to fit the stereotypes. The press has even convinced the American Indian Movement people that they are doing what is right and are champions of Indian causes. Everyone has heard of AIM, and most people are convinced that they represent the majority of the Indians in the country.

It is often asked, why don't the other Indian organizations speak out? They have spoken out, but nobody wants to listen to them because they aren't too dramatic or newsworthy. The only time they are even slightly listened to is when they are called on to react to one of the latest AIM antics.

But there are more serious reasons why there hasn't been more vocal objection: (1) It is an unwritten ethic that one Indian group does not attack another. (2) It isn't their goals that are objected to, but the methods used to obtain them, and there is always a possibility that the actions of AIM will call attention to real grievances and cause some needed change to come about.

It is time for the representatives of the government to meet with the real Indian leaders (tribal chairmen and others who have been seriously working for better Indian-government relationships for a number of years).

There should be a "once and for all" understanding about the treaty rights and the land-claim wrongs. Indian people should not be led to continue in the belief that the government owes them something and never meets its obligations. This attitude of expectancy has prevailed for over 100 years, and is not allowing the Indian people to attain their true potential.

If these changes do not come about, and the present formula of confrontation (with the media present), intimidation, destruction and reward continues to prevail, it will attract even more of the young people, and we can look for more to follow in the present direction taken by AIM.

Emily Peake, Minneapolis
Editor's note: The writer is executive director of the Upper Midwest American Indian Center in Minneapolis. [27]

The turmoil in the Minneapolis Indian community did not end there. No doubt youth programs were implemented at the Upper Midwest Center, but in these years any progress was "not enough." Emily's attention was increasingly drawn to the elders, the men and women to whom Indian people formerly gave the highest honors, now often poor and isolated in odd corners of the city. Especially the women, for generally the men died younger. Emily made it her personal mission to seek them out, introduce them to government services to which they were entitled, and generally bring them back into the Indian community. Why not a television program to accomplish this and more? Thus, together with her loyal ally Jim Longie—Chief Blackbird—she prevailed on WTCN Channel 11 to provide a slot for a weekly public service half-hour show—"Madagimo" (The Messenger). For eight years Emily and Jim alternately hosted "Madagimo." The program included weekly guests in an interview format interspersed with cultural history, even Native American legends dramatized by local actors. For sure the Upper Midwest American Indian Center was given exposure, but so was the Minneapolis American Indian Center, and any other organization or government agency that the hosts deemed of interest to the Indian community. In 1981, after Channel 11 was purchased by NBC, the public service slots were sacrificed in the interest of network programming. Thus did one tool for integrating an often-fractured community disappear.

Not Indian, Not White

Emily claimed to be Indian, but I never knew just exactly how. To me she
was always a white person. She was the most human person I have ever
met. She transcended any identification—Indian or white. She was open
and willing to try anything. She was happy all the time. She could step in
when there was strife and find a solution.
> —Larry Martin, Ojibwe full-blood

Who was Emily Peake? As a child she saw herself as "French and English"; in her early adult years she considered herself American, no hyphen. It was only after the Vienna debacle that Emily made an abrupt turn back to her family roots, and specifically to the roots deriving from her Ojibwe ancestors. One can imagine Emily saying to herself, "I shall take every skill I have learned in the melting pot and use it to bring about a better life for *my* people, the Ojibwe and our Native cousins, the Dakota." Emily's subsequent life was totally dedicated to this single purpose. She was eminently successful when it came to wheedling, educating, or otherwise influencing key elements of the non-Indian community. Sadly, she was not totally successful in persuading some of her fellow Native Americans as to her rightness. Emily had fierce followers. She also had doubters, even among the board and staff of the Upper Midwest Center. Just a year after the youth protest had been diffused, there occurred a more serious challenge to Emily's style. On March 13, 1974, some twenty pickets appeared outside the entrance to the Center. Most embarrassingly, they included both current and former staff members. Upper Midwest was a Model Indian Center, partially funded by the federal government, hence was required to have at least two-thirds of its eighteen-member board of directors be Indian. It wasn't that the board contained too many non-Indians; rather the "Indian" slots hadn't been filled. These and other complaints, all claiming that the Center was not responsive enough to its Indian clientele, were fully aired in the press. Staff member

Ignatia Broker* went so far as to say "We do not mind co-workers that are non-Indian. We are asking that the decisions be made by Indians. If this necessitates asking for the resignation of Emily Peake, then we will do that."[28]

Emily responded that the problems would be taken care of promptly. Yet she insisted on having the last word: "They thought all the people here should be American Indians." And that just wasn't Emily's way.

By 1975 Emily was gone from the Center, which didn't seem to deter her one bit. Time to devote more of her energies to the Indian elders. Minnesota had just signed on to a new Federal program—"communal dining"—or as it was initially called, "nutrition centers." Eventually there would be forty-two of these in Hennepin County. Yet too many Indian elders, many of them very needy, were reluctant to participate. Emily found a place for herself on the program staff and promptly made it her goal to bring these Indian elders out from their isolation. The place to start was St. Stephens Church in South Minneapolis, close to the center of the city's urban Indian community. If she could find an Indian woman to head this communal dining site, the Native elders would follow. So reasoned Emily. Her choice was Alberta Bedeau Norris, originally of Red Lake.

Emily had first encountered Alberta in 1970, when Alberta moved with her family to Minneapolis. A shy young woman, she had ventured into the tiny Upper Midwest office in South Minneapolis. "It was furnished like a living room, so friendly it was. I was so shy, I was afraid to talk to people. With Emily's encouragement I began to talk and I tried new things and I became more confident. Emily arranged for me to visit the State employment agency. They found me a part-time job and sent me to school."[29]

In 1975 Alberta Norris became director of the St. Stephens dining site, which soon became known as Indian-friendly and remains so to this day.

---

* Ignatia Broker, originally of White Earth, wrote one of the loveliest books of the twentieth century, a fictionalized memoir of an Ojibwe girl. The title: *Night Flying Woman*, cited in the bibliography.

Emily in Charge II

I'm really happy. We finally have the mortgage paid. The Indian
community is finally coming into its own. It has taken a while.
We're not there yet.
—Emily Peake, January 26, 1986

Among Emily Peake's many supporters in what locally were "high
places" was Minneapolis's sometime mayor Charles Stenvig. In fact,
a kind of symbiotic chemistry existed between these two strong
and sometimes controversial leaders. As happens with people in
politics, each had a cadré of loyal supporters. In the mayor's case,
it was the Minneapolis Police officers, for Charles Stenvig was first
and foremost a policeman. When one thinks back on the turmoil of
the late 1960s, it should come as no surprise that "law and order"
had become a large issue. In 1969, after a campaign in which the
local police union played a major role, Charles Stenvig had been
elected mayor of the city.

Yet the time came when Mayor Stenvig was voted out of office.
In late December of 1977, a few days before his term ended,
he presented Emily with Minneapolis's "Distinguished Citizen
Award."

Whether this award was the impetus or whether the motivation
was simply Emily's competence and enthusiasm, in 1978 she was
brought back from exile and rehired as executive director of the
Upper Midwest American Indian Center. The board that hired her
was almost totally "Indian." It did no harm that Emily's longtime ally
Jim Longie was Chairman.

What followed were a number of good years at the Upper
Midwest Center. Under Emily the Center became very skilled
in grantsmanship. Hy Rosen, Emily's colleague from the very
beginning, was now the designated off-board "advisor." He seemed

able to identify every federal program that came along and was able to provide the expertise as to how each one could be bent to benefit Minneapolis's minority populations. This was also the time when the three major Indian centers finally realized the necessity of moving closer to one another. Thus did MUID come into being—Minneapolis Urban Indian Directors—a triumvirate that included Irv Sargent, director of the Minneapolis American Indian Center, Vernell Wabasha, director of the Division of Indian Work under the Minneapolis Council of Churches, and Emily, director of the Upper Midwest Center. In the annals of urban Indian politics, this alliance was a breakthrough.* But the Seniors, the Indian elders, were increasingly the center of Emily's attention. Alberta Norris, once the shy young Indian woman from Red Lake, more recently Emily's alter ego in community dining centers, was once again on Emily's agenda. Where was Alberta? Back with her family at Red Lake caring for her aged father. Emily learned that he had died, hence sent a messenger up to Red Lake to retrieve this valuable ally. Alberta demurred, for her family had no place to live in the city. Emily went to work and found a remodeled house near the Upper Midwest Center. She even managed a VA mortgage for Alberta's veteran husband so that Alberta could become director of senior services at the Center. Eventually Alberta would move out to the suburbs and on to General Mills. No longer with the Center's staff, she was elected to the Board. One can only imagine how many other Native American life journeys were quietly orchestrated by the we-can-make-it-work magician Emily Peake.

In 1985 Emily was elected to the board of directors of the local Urban Coalition. Quite an honor this was, to be part of an organization that included the top executives of the city's major business and industrial firms, as well as leaders from the most radical black and Indian organizations (The Way and AIM). The Urban Coalition had been a bold experiment initiated just months after the 1966 destruction of Plymouth Avenue. Its first years were

* In 2003, MUID continues to function as a clearing house for ideas and programs among a number of local Indian service and lobbying organizations.

an experience in confrontation, with meetings that routinely verged on the chaotic. But the commitment was strong, the leadership often brilliant, and by 1985 the Urban Coalition was perhaps the most effective agent for change in Minneapolis.*

In January of 1986, at the annual meeting of the Upper Midwest American Indian Center, with Emily surrounded by a crowd of friends and supporters, Chief Blackbird burned the Center's mortgage. It had been twenty years since the initial funding allowed the Upper Midwest Center to purchase the building that now was entirely its own. And what an array of services emanated from its premises—not only a program for Seniors, but also a temporary daily labor pool, an Indian advocate from the county for help in accessing the county's systems, a legal aid attorney, a representative of city government to intervene when eviction threatened, and a child-welfare placement program.[30]

Not more than a few weeks after the celebration, Emily was voted out as director. It all happened at a board meeting, which for some reason Emily did not attend. There had always been some on the board, perhaps also on the staff, who were dissatisfied with Emily's style. Emily would have dismissed this as office politics, for her attention was always fixed on the Center's goals. Some recall that the Center was heavily in debt—spread too thin for the limited funds available. Whatever the reasons, in 1986 the Upper Midwest American Indian Center was no longer Emily's fief.

---

* In the year 2003 the board of the Urban Coalition includes representatives from the major business and industrial firms in the Twin Cities, from government, and from Black, Hispanic, Indian, and Asian community organizations. Its mission: "To increase the capacity of low-income African-American, American Indian, Asian Pacific and Chicano/Latino communities to address political, economic, and social concerns that are identified, and to promote the public dialogue through research-based advocacy and policy work."

Into the Mists

Time for Herself and Others

A tiny little thing with a great big presence.
—Judge Isabel Gomez, speaking of Emily
in Court as *Guardian ad Litem*

The message of forced retirement sent to Emily must have been a positive one, for she gave no indication of regret. Suddenly there was more time for twelve-year-old David, whom she had raised from infancy. It wasn't always easy, not for Emily and not for David, though she loved him dearly. In the mid-1980s David wasn't the only family offspring being raised by Emily. Jackie's three Heine sons all spent longer or shorter times with their Great Aunt Adieu. Jay was the oldest and soon out on his own, but both Grant and Scott would live with Emily in their teenage years, attending Central High School with all the promises and dangers this entailed. And still there was Natalie, grandmother to Jay, Scott, and Grant, great-grandmother to David. She was now seventy-two years old and had spent virtually her entire adult life in mental institutions. Emily arranged to have Natalie moved from Hastings State Hospital to a nursing home in Minneapolis. In all the years Emily had rarely missed a week of regular visits. Now it would be much more convenient, walking distance even, if she ever found it necessary to give up her auto. Time also for Emily to pursue what had long been on her mind—family genealogy, especially the curious roots of Caroline LeHavre Beaupre, from Mississippi (Grandma Carrie); a dictionary of Ojibwe names, beginning with Minnesota towns and lakes; a gathering and recording of Ojibwe legends; perhaps even a family memoir. But much of this would still have to be postponed, for Emily's evenings and weekends were not yet her own.*

It wasn't long after retirement that Emily was placed in the *Guardian ad Litem* pool at Hennepin County District Court. This

was a volunteer position to represent the interests of individual children who come under the Court's protective custody. In her time, Emily was the only Indian *Guardian ad Litem* in the county. Yet every Indian child that came under her wing received her fierce commitment, no less than the commitment she had earlier made to Jackie,

**David Peake & his great great aunt
Adieu, 1986**

to Evon, and to Suzie when they were children, and now to David, to Grant, and to Scott. It seemed that Emily had been born to be a *Guardian ad Litem*. She had the capacity to get to know the families of the children under her protection, without compromising the safety and the interests of the children themselves. So well did this difficult role fit her make-up.

But then fate suddenly called "Halt!" Just a year after leaving the Upper Midwest American Indian Center Emily Peake was diagnosed with breast cancer. She promptly underwent a mastectomy. Following a regimen of chemotherapy, Emily's prognosis was good. Life could go forward again, including her myriad responsibilities—Emily called them "opportunities"—but now with a fresh sense of urgency as well as a sharper focus on resolving conflicts. Time on

---

* In these years Emily Peake served on the National Indian Council on Aging, the Minnesota Board on Aging, the Urban Coalition, and the Minnesota Indian Historical Society, of which she was a founder.

this earth was finite and certainly not to be wasted, especially when it came to the most vulnerable—the children and the elderly.

Using her grant-writing skills, which in the Upper Midwest Center years had become legendary, Emily crafted a proposal to the State of Minnesota. She chose as her accomplice Amie Flocken, namesake of Emily's mother Louise and colleague in many previous efforts on behalf of their people. The two women proposed to travel in the northland and determine the needs of rural Indian elders through personal interviews. The grant was awarded, and off they went to places like Cass Lake, White Earth, Bena, Bemidji, and beyond. At Bemidji they found Ignatia Broker, by then a well-known Minnesota Indian author. From her and from others they learned about isolation, lack of transportation, medical problems, loneliness, and other ailments of many elderly, Indian and non-Indian alike. Afterward, with data in hand, they pestered the State Legislature to fund an "Indian desk" at the Minnesota Board of Aging. So persuasive was Emily in political circles that when she visited the legislature, it was difficult to say no. Indeed the funds were granted.

Time for Emily to turn back to her own neighborhood, now threatened with permanent decay, for in the 1970s Stevens Square was riddled with drugs. In fact, the lovely hillock park that defined the neighborhood was serving as a center of wider drug commerce.

Emily's Neighborhood

I've been here long enough to become a senior citizen, and now that is one
of my interests. If we don't have a safe neighborhood where people can go
out to the grocery store... we don't have anything.
—Emily Peake at a neighborhood meeting,
June 18, 1992

Stevens Square Neighborhood can easily be defined. It begins just
south of the I-94 freeway, essentially overlooking the Minneapolis
Convention Center. The area stretches from Nicollet Avenue on the
west to the I-35W freeway on the east. The southern boundary is
Franklin Avenue. In the center of the little neighborhood lies the
block-size Stevens Square park, named for Colonel John Stevens,
an early pioneer. Most of the buildings in the blocks surrounding
the park were, and remain, three-and-a-half story brick apartment
buildings, erected between 1912 and 1919. They were built with
small, moderately priced rental units, within walking distance
of the city center. So they are to this day. The neighborhood also
includes several institutions and a handful of single-family homes
that have survived the wrecker's ball. Among these is 1919 Second
Avenue, Emily's home from 1970 on.

In the late 1960s, when the area was declining precipitously, a
local entrepreneur, John Larson, began an extensive rehabilitation
of the brick apartment buildings. General Mills also invested
in the rehabilitation effort, believing that the Stevens Square
neighborhood was worth "saving." Thanks to committed residents
and property owners who cared, the Stevens Square Community
Organization was born. An early priority was the effort to designate
the buildings surrounding the park as a "historic district" and bring
them under Minneapolis's Preservation code. Emily understood

well how to penetrate city government bureaucracy and reach the power center. When the designation finally came through in 1990, she was pleased to declare:

> *I worked on [the designation] a long time. I'm very, very happy that we got it. Designation as a historic district makes it a more stable and interesting place. People can say they are proud to live in a historic place, not in a drug neighborhood.*[31]

Emily was a mainstay of the Stevens Square Community Organization, SSCO as it has come to be known. Over the years she served as chair of the community safety committee and vice chair of the Board. She wrote the application that resulted in a grant from the Headwaters Foundation, money to hire a community crime prevention coordinator. Indeed Emily had a serious stake in neighborhood safety. At age seventy she was caregiver and temporary parent to a baby and three teenagers. Only one of them belonged to her—fourteen-year-old David. The others? Just runaway children, one with a child of her own, who knew that Emily would always take them in.

By 1992 the Stevens Square Community Organization had acquired more than a little clout. Now the recipient of annual funds from the city's Neighborhood Revitalization Program, the organization could support an office and a paid staff. Drugs were no longer a piece of the park landscape. Rather, the Minneapolis Park Board had installed new playground equipment, new wrought-iron benches, shrubs, and beds of flowers. Even a performance stage was in the offing. Yet a general uneasiness prevailed when 160 residents and property owners* attended the June annual meeting. Besides election of officers and board members, the principal issue on the agenda was a proposal by the Central Community

---

* Minneapolis neighborhood designations combined Stevens Square with Loring Heights, also bounded by I-94 and Franklin Avenue. Loring Heights ranged west from Nicollet to Lyndale Avenue. If east of Nicollet was "poverty to moderate," then west of Nicollet was "moderate to affluent." Both sections included commercial property and institutions. In 2003 not much has changed.

Housing Trust (CCHT) to turn a vacant apartment building at 1801 LaSalle Avenue into transitional housing for the homeless. Months earlier, the proposal had been voted down overwhelmingly by the Stevens Square Housing Development Committee and then by the Board. Still the Housing Trust was going forward with its plans. Emily and others spoke against the proposal, citing the urgency of moving the neighborhood toward increased stability and security. This annual meeting is long remembered by those who attended. Emily's presence is also vividly recalled—"a gentle, peacemaking soul" in the midst of an assemblage frustrated that the will of the neighborhood counted for so little.*

Unfinished Business

In May of 1990 Natalie Peake Blanch died. She was seventy-six years old and had spent a half century in institutions of one kind or another. Natalie was deeply mourned by sister Emily and daughter Jackie, not so much for her passing, but rather for her gentle nature and creative spirit that had been crushed by mental illness. Natalie's remains were buried next to those of her father in St. Paul's Acacia Cemetery. He too had been felled by mental illness in the prime of his life.

That summer, partly as a tribute to Natalie and their mother, Emily proposed a major study that would encompass Indian history from earliest times to the present day. The vehicle for all of this would be research into "Life Styles of Ojibwe Women in

---

* The Central Community Housing Trust proposal was eventually implemented, with the promise of twenty-four-hour support services and adequate building security. In 2003 "The Coyle" apartments at 1801 LaSalle are fully occupied, though the twenty-four-hour support services ceased long ago. Over the years, the neighborhood and the Trust have worked together to keep "The Coyle" apartments a safe place for the residents and for the neighborhood. It is a continuing challenge.[31]

Minnesota—Traditional, Transitional, and Contemporary." Her hope was to reconcile the contradictions that go with living in and between two cultures. Emily submitted her proposal to the Minnesota Historical Society. It was well received and fully funded. The project started out well. Emily interviewed Winnie Jourdain, one of Minnesota's great Native American matriarchs. Thanks to the quality of both interviewer and interviewee, it turned out to be a most insightful piece of autobiography. Unfortunately all that survives of "Life Styles of Ojibwe Women" is the Winnie Jourdain essay and a fragment interview with Ignatia Broker, both on file at the Minnesota Historical Society. Perhaps with Emily's impatience to fix all that needed fixing in the world, there was simply too little time for reflection.

Back in 1980 Emily's old friend Hy Rosen had founded the Greater Lake Country Food Bank on an obscure street in the near north side of Minneapolis. Hy, once a grocer himself, knew the sources of goods. In fact, he was a near genius in acquiring donated commodities from the basic to the gourmet. From the very beginning, Emily was involved. By 1990 she was spending almost full time at Hy's food bank, figuring out where to distribute the food—senior apartment buildings, charter schools, day-care centers, drop-in centers, shelters of every kind. Both she and her loyal friend Jim Longie* served on the board. Together they had become the two principal volunteers.

In 1993 Emily's cancer returned, this time as liver cancer. The prognosis was not good, but she and the medical profession would give it their best. Emily began a series of chemotherapy treatments at the University Hospital. It was Jim Longie who weekly delivered her to the hospital and waited to return her home. On other weekdays it was Jim Longie who picked Emily up and brought her to the Greater Lake Country Food Bank. Together they sorted, made phone calls, scheduled pickups, and did whatever was necessary to facilitate the daily food distribution. It seemed the sicker Emily became, the more

---

* Chief Blackbird, who with Emily was a piece of the Upper Midwest American Indian Center from the beginning.

of her energies she devoted to this food bank that served the elders and the children.

In between these excursions Emily was mostly at home, alone, happy to entertain those who stopped by, but without the energy to take them in. Much of her time she spent at her desk in the little back room of her house—her office, she called it. Yes, the desk, cov-

ered with papers out of a past more remote than her own lifetime, papers outlining projects, and papers containing visions far beyond what was achievable in the time left.

But the world was not yet done with Emily. She was searching for something that had long been in the back of her

**Evon Mims Shahan & her great aunt
Adieu, 1986**

mind. There had always been rumors in the neighborhood, rumors that dated from the Cold War, something about the Army spraying the neighborhood with chemicals from trucks and even sending a foreign chemical through the air ducts of Clinton School, where Emily had volunteered so often after returning from Europe. Was it possible that her cancer had its origin in these military pranks? Such was her question, initially to herself and subsequently to Minnesota's Senator Paul Wellstone. Late in 1993, she called on Senator Wellstone in his office and laid out before him the rumors that still ran through the community. The senator agreed to look into the issue, and indeed he did. What he discovered was that the rumors were true. During the Cold War, the United States Army had conducted experiments in Minneapolis and elsewhere in Minnesota.

Months after Wellstone's request, the army released to him the forty-one-year-old reports. In 1953, over a period of several months, zinc cadmium sulfide had been sprayed over Minneapolis neighborhoods and into buildings, especially Clinton School, which had had multiple attacks. Altogether ninety-one chemical releases occurred in the city, fifty-two of these between January 19 and April 28, thirty-nine between August 21 and September 18. According to these reports, the Army had obtained approval from the city's mayor by assuring him that the chemicals used were of an "inert material . . . a simulant having no viability," in other words "completely harmless." However, the 1953 report also stated that "the size range of the material employed approximates that which is considered most effective in penetrating into the lungs."[32]

Clearly, Emily's visit with her senator had opened a hornet's nest. Subsequent hearings were held in Minneapolis, with testimony from former students of Clinton Elementary School. A number of those giving testimony had suffered chronic illnesses of one kind or another in the intervening four decades. The Army mounted an investigation while Congress authorized the National Academy of Sciences to conduct a full assessment of the chemical.* And Emily? She was now tethered to a portable oxygen tank.

The time came when Emily could not leave the house alone. Yet Hy Rosen, like Jim Longie, refused to let go: "I would take Emily out to lunch from time to time. I'd drive over to her little house. We'd load her oxygen tank into my car, then drive to a little restaurant on Nicollet Avenue. Those were wonderful days."

---

* *Toxicologic Assessment of the Army's Zinc Cadmium Sulfide Dispersion Tests: Answers to Commonly Asked Questions*, National Academy Press, Washington, D.C., 1997.

Alcohol

One-third of the 45,000 Indians in Minnesota have chemical dependency
problems. And those one-third are related to the other two-thirds. The
whole family is involved with the illness. . . . If we leave it untreated, we'll
have another generation of children growing up with the same problems.
—Andy Favorite, Director, American
Indian Chemical Diversion Project[33]

In 1981 a paper entitled "A Ten-Year Follow-Up of Alcoholic Native Americans in Minnesota" was presented at the annual meeting of the American Psychiatric Association and later published in the prestigious *American Journal of Psychiatry*. The authors: Dr. Joseph Westermeyer, M.D., Ph.D., Department of Psychiatry at the University of Minnesota, and Emily Peake of the Upper Midwest American Indian Center in Minneapolis. It is not clear exactly what Emily's role in the study was. It may well have been to locate and interview forty-five Native Americans who ten years earlier had been patients at the University of Minnesota Hospital—patients with severe, life-threatening alcohol problems. At that time, each of these patients had been counseled and placed in an appropriate rehabilitation program.

Over the decade, nine of the forty-five former patients had died and one could not be located. Of the thirty-five who were interviewed, seven had improved and were self-supporting, seven continued in the lifestyle of the previous decade, including interludes of alcohol treatment, and nineteen were in worse shape than they had been ten years earlier. A summary of the conclusions was also published.

"The authors hypothesize that the absence of stable employment and a stable marriage or family environment reduced the efficacy of treatment efforts in this population. Those who achieved two years of abstinence were characterized by stable employment and/or marriage, as well as by stronger interpersonal relationships and less depression than the others. The recovered subjects provided considerable help to other alcoholic persons, in addition to serving as positive role models."[34]

For all of the care the original forty-five subjects received during their hospitalization and afterward, and for all of the money invested in the study, the final conclusions were hardly new and somehow simplistic. Probably Emily initially bought into the conclusions. What seems clear, however, is that in her last years she went well beyond that which came out of the study. After 1987 Emily Peake, once of the Minnesota Melting Pot, wanted desperately to understand the unique spiritual dimension that goes with "being Indian." She began seriously to study the Chippewa language, looked into the legends, all toward plumbing the soul of her people in the hope of finding a clue to the alcoholism that routinely destroyed almost a fourth of the Native American population. Even Emily's enduring dream of an Indian village next to Old Fort Snelling had its origins in her passion to capture the children as they grew to adolescence. Like Old Fort Snelling, the village would be a "museum" under the Minnesota Historical Society. Like Old Fort Snelling, it would be staffed mostly by young people. In Emily's village these young people would be Dakota and Ojibwe, learning their own history and its underlying spiritual dimension while proudly sharing their heritage with others. The sicker Emily became, the more intense was her vision of the Indian village—an alternative to boredom, hopelessness, depression, and alcohol.

The village was unfinished business in Emily's own life journey. However, it may yet find resonance among today's Native American leaders and other role models in the Indian community. A cursory glance at the leaders, both urban and rural, reveals a disproportionate number of recovering alcoholics. Some have visited treatment centers, others not. Most of these men and women probably do fit the description of successful recovery as detailed in the Westermeyer/Peake study, though this would be less the cause than the effect of their continuing recovery.

The common element among these leading men and women appears to be a return to the "Indian religion." At White Earth and among the urban Ojibwe, "Indian religion" generally means some form of the Midewiwin, or Grand Medicine, as it was universally practiced before the arrival of the Christian missionaries. Midewiwin remains by nature a very personal journey among initiated brethren, cloaked in secrecy as it has been for the last five hundred years or so. It is sufficient here to say that the knowledge and disciplines gained from true Midewiwin are increasingly healing broken lives.

Recalling Emily's vision, what an impact might Indian history with its unique underpinning of "Indian religion" have on young people, especially in the environment of an Indian village next to Old Fort Snelling, where such a village did indeed once stand.

White Buffalo Calf Woman

There is a beautiful legend out of Lakota* history that regularly reappears in the literature, transcending tribe, race, and nation. In Emily's last year, as cancer gradually took over more and more of her body, she took this legend onto herself.

Many generations ago, two Lakota men out on a buffalo hunt came upon a newly born white buffalo calf. When the calf saw the men, she rolled over and stood up. Lo and behold, she had taken the form of a beautiful young Indian woman. In her brief encounter with the hunters this calf-turned-woman made a number of prophecies that were passed along from generation to generation, even up to the present. In our time Joseph Chasing Horse is the keeper of these prophecies. White Buffalo Calf Woman promised she will one day come again as a white calf. That calf will soon change color from white to yellow to reddish brown and black, and when the time comes that all races become reconciled with one another, the calf will change color from black to reddish brown to yellow to white and White Buffalo Calf Woman will appear once more.

---

* The "Great Sioux Nation" comprises the Dakota, the Lakota, and the Nakota language groups.

From time to time in the years a white buffalo calf has appeared here and there where Native people pay attention. Most of these calves have died even before making the full change from white to black. Those who understand the prophecy continue to be patient, believing that in due time the prophecy will be fulfilled.[35]

In the summer of 1994, Emily's last summer, such a buffalo calf did appear. She was born on the farm of Dave and Valerie Heider near Janesville, Wisconsin. The Heiders named the calf "Miracle." News of Miracle's birth soon traveled the nation. American Indians of every tribe, and non-Indians as well, made a hurried pilgrimage to the Heider farm. Always the fear was that Miracle would die before achieving her initial miraculous color change.

When Emily heard the news, she was frantic. She must gather all the Indian children who lived in the city and take them to Miracle. There they would indeed feel the power of White Buffalo Calf Woman's prophecies. Emily needed to look no further than her oxygen tank to know that she was powerless in the matter. She still had her telephone, though, and she did the next best thing. Clyde Bellecourt, that worthy opponent in earlier battles, was the one man who could make it happen. Besides, he and she shared the crane dodem. Emily phoned Clyde—"You rent the bus and I'll find the children."[36]

Perhaps the time was not right; perhaps it was a foolish idea after all. Seven years later, Clyde Bellecourt doesn't remember the conversation. Why should he? His phone rings day and night, year in and year out. Clyde does remember Emily, however. "She was a good woman. I liked her."

Miracle is alive and well, having attained her black color as prophesied by White Buffalo Calf Woman. She still plays hostess to streams of visitors, both at the Heider farm and on her Web site. According to those who believe, when all the races do become reconciled with one another, Miracle's color will change from black to reddish brown to yellow to white, and White Buffalo Calf Woman will appear once more.

Early in April of 1995, Jackie moved into Emily's home. Jackie intended to care for her aunt as Emily had once cared for her, and later her daughters, her sons, and her grandson.

Word spread quickly that Emily Peake's days were numbered. Arne Carlson, Governor of Minnesota, was the first to respond by proclaiming an "Emily Peake Day" throughout the state. At the national capitol, in a rare show of bipartisanship, Representatives Jim Ramstad and Martin Sabo read into the Congressional Record a joint tribute to Emily Peake. Just in time. On the sixteenth of the month it all seemed to be coming down. Jackie was very frightened. She rushed Emily to University Hospital. Emily spent the night in the hospital but refused to stay any longer—"no more oxygen, I want to go home."

Jackie brought Emily home and sat with her throughout that last night. It was an extraordinary experience. Emily lay with her hands outstretched upward. At first she was calling for her doctor, but then she appeared to change her mind.

> *Don't touch me—God help me—Don't touch one thing.*
> *God's got me. Leave me alone.*
> *O.K. Let's go. Pull it up, way up. O.K. Pull it up. Pick me up.*
> *Open the door—Get me out.*[37]

And then she died. The date: April 18, 1995.

All that Remains

Those who knew Emily, and perhaps those who only read her column in
this paper, are experiencing a sense of loss. . . . In fact, it's difficult to
talk about her in the past tense, because the future tense fits her better.
She would call to say, 'Let's plan an award dinner, and we will give those
children some recognition—they don't get enough' or 'I hope to finish my
place name translation dictionary soon—I'll be over to work on it today.'
. . . Anyone who ever was at a public event where Emily was present knows
that she was the go-between for people, families and communities. Getting
people to talk and laugh together is something she could do and often did.
We'll all miss her and miss what she did so well.

—The Editor: *The Spirit*, American
Indian OIC,* May 1995

In accordance with Emily's wishes, her body was cremated. Jackie
and her three sons carried the ashes up to White Earth. At St.
Columba Church, the priest conducted a graveside service in which
he deplored the modern custom of cremation. With that admonition
to vex them, the four mourners placed the urn containing Adieu's
ashes in the ground next to the final resting place of her mother.
A few weeks later Jackie visited her aunt's grave once more, this
time accompanied by daughter Evon and son Grant. Together they
installed a permanent white marble monument over Emily's buried
urn, some four feet up a slight incline from Louise's headstone.
Engraved on the polished marble surface are the words "In loving
memory of Emily 'Adieu' Peake." Connecting the monument
with Louise's headstone is a pair of black wrought iron fences. In
summer a bed of colorful annuals completes this miniature walled

---

* The American Indian Opportunity Industrialization Center is a center for
technology training based on the philosophy of Reverend Leon Sullivan of
Philadelphia. From 1978 through 1994, Emily Peake wrote a monthly column
for *The Spirit*.

garden. Thus the Peake burial spot—mother and daughter—has become a high point for travelers who choose to visit the stunning St. Columba Mission Church, itself a masterpiece of variegated quarried stone, and the "old Indian cemetery" that surrounds it.

Some days after the burial of Emily's ashes, a memorial service was held in the hall of the Upper Midwest Indian Center. Estimates of those present range from 200 to 300, many of whom signed the Guest Book. They included elected officials at every level, two family court judges, and citizens from every corner of the community and of every race, color, and creed. A drummer and singer set the stage. Many stood and gave testimony to the goodness of Emily Peake and to her impact on their lives. One could swear that at least on this particular day, Emily Peake *was* the White Buffalo Calf Woman.

Eight years later: The White Earth Ojibwe Reservation, where Emily's roots as well as her remains are buried, has come on better times. The tribal coffers have benefited greatly from the Shooting Star Casino at Mahnomen. The tribe now operates two schools and has recently established the White Earth Tribal and Community College. Direct benefits to the residents come in the form of more jobs—at the casino and in tribal programs. The unemployment rate has dropped from eighty-five percent to fifty-six percent. In spite of limited opportunities and chronic poverty, tribal members are returning to the reservation. As it has always been and no doubt will always be, White Earth is "home."

In Minneapolis, the two great Indian Centers that owe their beginnings to Emily Peake are both thriving. The Upper Midwest American Indian Center is now located in a former bank building on the corner of Broadway and Emerson Avenue North. It barely resembles the early institution that supported itself with monthly potlucks and powwows. The Center serves some 3,000 Indian people annually, having evolved into an emporium of Indian family services, all coordinated by director Gertrude Buckanaga, once of White Earth. Each service program is separately funded—Head

Start for preschoolers, Foster Care and Adoption for children of every age, after-school Enrichment, Mental Health services, adult education in Life Skills, and the Four Directions Charter High School, founded by the Center but now independent. On the agenda for the near future is a culturally based Wellness Center, and beyond that a proposal for affordable housing.

Over on East Franklin Avenue, the Minneapolis American Indian Center provides a phalanx of programs and services—a mentoring program for teenagers, a senior citizens program, adult education classes toward earning a high school equivalence degree, wellness education, a chemical dependency program, and a pool of advocates for those dealing with the social welfare system. The Two Rivers Gallery at the Center has earned a place in Twin Cities cultural life, with a permanent collection of contemporary Native American art plus rotating exhibits throughout the year. Under the leadership of director Frances Fairbanks, the Center is working through the third year of a five-year Strategic Plan.

Tucked away on the near north side, the Greater Lake Country Food Bank continues to gather and dispense mountains of packaged food to the community of need. Hy Rosen, still CEO of the operation, manages it all from his tiny office. To call on Hy one must first pass through the outer office, where the visitor is greeted by a large framed photo mounted on the wall—a portrait of Emily Peake in her most active years.

Emily's friendship circle, accumulated over a lifetime, is amazingly intact. All four of her closest childhood friends are still with us—Frances Anderson in Chicago and the three surviving Belladettes in suburban Minneapolis. Unfortunately Inez Sandness—Iney of Emily's childhood—can no longer speak. This writer visited Inez recently and asked her to write down words that would best describe Emily Peake. Inez took a pen and in a difficult scrawl wrote the words "patient" and "fun loving." Emily's family would agree. The incomparable Adieu—as she was known to Jackie and her children—was above all patient and fun loving.

Larry Martin, who best remembers Emily from her early volunteer days at Waite House, speaks of how beautiful she was, with her hair pulled back in the high style of European fashion. Not long ago Jackie had a dream. Adieu was coming through a revolving door, elegantly dressed, with her long black hair tied in back, as Jackie remembered from her childhood. Adieu smiled at Jackie but continued through the revolving door back whence she came.

Besides these memories and many more, there is also the Emily Peake Memorial Garden.

Emily Peake
undated photo by Evon Shahan

Afterword

It is finished, this tale of Emily Peake, the Ojibwe mixed-blood. I never encountered Emily in her lifetime, yet I now have a vivid picture of her etched in my mind's eye. My hope is that you, dear reader, likewise will remember Emily Peake. For me, that is reward enough.

Yet after all I have learned of the history and culture that molded Emily and her kind, I still do not understand what it is "to be Indian." Perhaps that is the wonder of it all—that we who have not grown up in the Indian culture will *never* really know. We shall never be able to comprehend the pride, the contradictions, the treasures, and indeed the tragedies that are reincarnated one way or another in every generation.

In my relative ignorance as an outsider, I yet dare to share with you my take on the matter. I believe it all goes back to *the land*— that sanctified treasure granted eons ago to these "first people" by their deity. No matter how much money is invested in native communities by casinos, foundations, churches, and government agencies; no matter how successful Indian elders are in passing on to coming generations the language, the lore, the arts, the history, and the religion unique to their tribe; no matter how many young people complete high school, even college and professional schools—the tragedies and trauma besetting much of the Indian community will not go away. All of the above notwithstanding, the *loss* of the land is the overwhelming trauma, unconsciously passed on from generation to generation.

Among the White Earth Ojibwe, whether or not they dwell on the reservation, this loss is today being addressed in bits and pieces. Whenever land that was once part of the greater reservation area becomes available at a price the tribe can afford, it competes to snatch up the parcel with funds found here and there in the tribal coffers. Usually these are small parcels, tax-forfeited land and not the choicest. However, in 2001, when 40 acres of prime rice marsh came on the market, the tribe found the funds to purchase it, thus increasing its meager landholdings.

More interesting to those outside the Indian community is the tax-exempt foundation created in 1989 by Winona Leduc of White Earth. Its name: White Earth Land Recovery project; its address: Ponsford, Minnesota 56575. Although the programs supported by this project are not restricted to land purchase, the underlying purpose of the foundation is the acquisition of lost land. To date, 1,500 acres of White Earth land have been purchased, some of it then donated to the tribe, the rest used for other project purposes. Contributions are more than welcome. Funds designated "for land purchase" go directly to the "land fund."

JANE PEJSA SEPTEMBER 2003

Appendix A
Friday Girl Promotional Piece, 1956

$Friday$

FEderal 6-8947

308 LUMBER EXCHANGE, MINNEAPOLIS 1

Translations • Secretarial Services • Convention Coverage

Dear Sir:

The old saying, "The written word is the word that lives" is as true today as it ever was, and the information that is so carefully prepared and delivered at your more important meetings and conventions should not be allowed to die.

Many a carefully prepared speech containing vital information has been lost in the smoke of a convention hall. However, just suppose we had optimum conditions such as a well ventilated hall with everyone present in an alert, attentive audience--even in such an unusual situation (after the usual number of speeches) only a fraction of the messages would be remembered the next day, and less the next week.

The advantages of a written message are manifold. Not only does a written message refresh the memory, but it often reveals ideas that were missed, or only half understood, at the time of presentation. It gives the delegate, or reader, the opportunity of mulling over the ideas at his leisure and organizing them into an effective meaningful presentation to the group awaiting his report.

What I am leading up to is this -- we now have a new service to offer you. You may now have your speeches recorded (at a price less than it would cost you to rent a recorder) and transcribed (at regular stenographic rates). We will also have printed any number of speeches you designate for your group at a price per copy well within the reach of each member.

We realize the importance of time in such instances, and will try to get the finished work to you as quickly as possible.

This service is also available for your smaller group meetings where question and answer periods prove very valuable.

Enclosed is a post card for your convenience. I would appreciate your returning it.

Automatically, your gal,

FRIDAY

P.S. Reservations also will be taken for meetings in the coming year (1957)

Appendix B

Upper Midwest American Indian Center
Selections from the Articles of Incorporation,
1961

Article I.

The name of this corporation shall be: Upper Midwest American Indian Center.

Article II.

The Purpose of this corporation shall be:

(a) To preserve and perpetuate the heritage of the American Indian and promote good citizenship.

(b) To further the educational, social, and cultural activities of the American Indian people.

(c) To promote the affiliation of American Indians of all tribes and their non-Indian friends into an educational, civic, and cultural organization, which is non-political and non-sectarian.

(d) To promote fellowship among the American Indian people of all tribes and to create bonds of understanding and fellowship between Indians and non-Indians.

(e) To assist Indians and their families to become assimilated into the modern urban social structure, *if they so desire.**

(f) To foster the educational and economic advancement of the American Indian people.

(g) To encourage artistic and avocational pursuits by American Indian people.

(h) To preserve and foster American Indian arts, crafts and cultural values.

(i) To encourage and engage generally in any courses or objects similar to the above-mentioned in order to promote the social, cultural, and educational welfare of the members and such

---

* The words "if they so desire" were added to the Articles in a 1967 amendment signed by James S. Longie, president of the corporation, and Emily Peake, secretary of the Corporation.

other purposes as are now or may hereafter be granted by the Minnesota Non-Profit Corporation Act.

Article VI.
The name of each incorporator of this corporation is: Fred Benjamin, Fred Blessing, Daniel W. Hardy, Frank Hurd, Louise Hurd, Emily Peake.*

Article VII.
The number of directors constituting the first Board of Directors of this corporation shall be eight (8) and the tenure of office of each such board of directors shall be one (1) year or until successors are elected and qualify.

The names of the board of directors are: Daniel W. Hardy, James Longie, Ray Deere, Florence Jones, Louise Hurd, Dell F. Cloutier, Mrs. Henry Larson, Emily Peake.

---

* The Articles of Incorporation were signed June 9, 1961, by each of the incorporators.

Appendix C
Promotional Piece for a UMAIC Program, 1967

NEWS FLASH

from the Upper Midwest American Indian Center

ATTENTION KIDS 6-12!

Little Susie Squirrel had been born into a long line of very active, adventurous, fun-loving (and often very mischievous) squirrels. In fact, when Susie had fallen into Charlie Chipmunk's dugout doorway while she had been scampering off with Sam Squirrel's acorns, no one in the forest had been surprised. While they had held her by the tail in order to dislodge the acorns which had jammed within her mouth during her accident, they recalled what her grandfather Sargent Squirrel had done over 50 years before. Grandfather Squirrel had spent his life teasing and tormenting the West Wind until one day old West Wind had come and had swept him straight into a big lake where he became a squirrel pool. And if you go to that big lake you will find, even today, Grandfather Squirrel swirling round and

round
and
round.

Realizing that little Susie Squirrel might get into the same vicious circle, her family and friends decided they'd better find something with which to keep her out of mischief. They heard of the Summer Youth Program at the Upper Midwest American Indian Center and decided to send her over to the Center on June 26 with Tommy Turtle, Priscilla Porcupine, and Fanny Fawn. In fact, all the kids in the forest were going to the Center that Monday morning and every day after that where they would play games, hear stories, paint, play with wood, and do ALL KINDS OF FUN THINGS!

Susie Squirrel and her friends invite all of you to play every day from the 26th on with her at the Upper Midwest American Indian

Center (if you live in North Minneapolis) or at the Waite House (if you live in South Minneapolis.)

AND if you come to the Center nearest you every day for the whole summer, Susie Squirrel MIGHT—JUST MIGHT—even take you to the big lake to see her grandfather's squirrel pool!

NOW REMEMBER!

All of you between the ages of 6 -12 are invited to either the Upper Midwest American Indian Center or the Waite House (whichever is nearest your home) on Monday, June 26, & all day every day for the whole summer!

GAMES, ARTS and CRAFTS, SWIMMING, etc.

Appendix D

"The 38 Dakota who sacrificed their lives for the Dakota
people, Mankato, Minnesota, December 26, 1862" *

Tipi Hdonica: One Who Forbids His House
Ptan Duta: Red Otter
Taoyata: His People
Hinhansa Koyagmani: One Who Walks Clothed In An Owl's Tail
Maza Bodu: Iron Blower
Wahpe Duta: Red Leaf
Sdodye Sni: meaning unknown
Hda Ya Mani: Tinkling Walker
Tate Hmi Yanyan: Round Wind
Hdaya Inyanka: Rattling Runner
Dowan Sa: The Singer
Hepan: Second Child, a Son
Sunka Ska: White Dog
Tunka Siku Icahda Mani: One Who Walks By His Grandfather
Ite Duta: Red Face
Kabdeca: Broken To Pieces
Hepi: Third Child, a Son
Mahpiya Akan Najin: One Who Stands on a Cloud
Hanke Dakota: A Half Breed
Caske: The First Born, a Son
Hanke Dakota: A Half Breed
Tate Ka Ga: Wind Maker
He Inkpa: The Tip Of The Horn
Hanke Dakota: A Half Breed
Nape Sni: One Who Does Not Flinch
Wakan Tanka: Great Spirit

---

* From "The U.S.-Dakota Conflict of 1862, a Self-Guided Tour," a brochure
published by the Mankato Area Chamber & Convention Bureau, Mankato,
Minnesota.

Tunkasitkulkiyena Najin: One Who Stands Close
  To His Grandfather
Maka Akan Najin: One Who Stands On The Earth
Wakute Wiyaya Mani: One Who Walks Prepared To Shoot
Aicage: To Grow Upon
Hotaninku: Voice That Appears Coming
Cetan Hunku: The Parent Hawk
Cankahda: Near The Wood
Hda Hiu Dan: To Make A Rattling Noise Suddenly
Oyate Aku: The Coming People
Howema-u: He Comes For Me
Wakinyan Cistina: Little Thunder
Tate Hdihoni: Wind Comes Home

Appendix E

Awards Presented to Emily Peake, 1980-1995

- Certificate of Appreciation presented by **WTCN Television, Inc**. to Emily Peake for her valued service on Channel 11's Program Advisory Committee. Signed by Robert C. Fransen, Vice President and General Manager, undated.

- Certificate of Recognition awarded by the **Central Community Council** to Emily Peake in recognition of her special achievements as a neighborhood volunteer. Unsigned, no date.

- Citation of Honor awarded by the **Hennepin County Board of Commissioners** to Emily Peake for 30 years of distinguished service to Hennepin County. Signed by Sam S. Sivanich, Commissioner, November 23, 1981.

- Certificate of Appreciation awarded to Emily Peake in recognition of Volunteer service to the **Hennepin County Department of Court Services**. Signed April 22, 1986, by Robert A. Forsythe, Chief Judge of the 4th Judicial District, and others.

- Certificate of Appreciation awarded by **St. Joseph's Home for Children** to Emily Peake as a Centennial Volunteer in recognition of her demonstrated commitment. Signed by Douglas H. Goke, June 22, 1986.

- Certificate from **Three Feathers Associates of Norman, Oklahoma**, stating that Emily Peake successfully completed a course of intensive training in sexual abuse of children and youth, focusing on incestuous families. Signed by Dona E. Doran and others, July 10, 1986.

- Certificate of Appreciation awarded by **Indian Family Services, Inc.** to Emily Peake for volunteering her time and services. Signed by Patrick Furrier, Chairperson, and Betty Greese, Director, August 27, 1986.

- Certificate acknowledging Emily Peake's supportive efforts to the **National Indian Council on Aging.** Signed by Sherman Lillead, September 1986.

- Certificate of Appreciation presented by the **City of Minneapolis** to Emily Peake in recognition of her outstanding volunteer service. Signed Alice W. Rainville, President City Council, and Don Fraser, Mayor, 1986.

- Certificate of Recognition presented by the **Opportunities Industrialization Centers of America, Inc.** to Emily Peake for active cooperation and participation on the Youth Career Awareness Committee. Signed by Leon H. Sullivan, Founder and Chairman, and by Elton Jolly, President and CEO, June 20, 1988.

- Certificate of Appreciation presented by the **Metropolitan Council of the Twin Cities Area** to Emily Peake for her distinguished service to the citizens of the Twin Cities Area. Signed by Steve Keefe, Chair, December 2, 1988.

- Certificate of Award presented by the **Urban Coalition of Minneapolis** to Emily Peake, in recognition of her distinguished service to the community as Director of the Urban Coalition from 1985 to 1989. Signed by the Chair of the Board of Directors, and by Yusef Mgeni, President, September 20, 1989.

- Certificate of Appreciation awarded by **The Minnesota Chippewa Tribe** to Emily Peake in recognition of her outstanding delivery of service to Indian Children and Families. Signed by Adrienne Bendix and Gary S. Frazer, Executive Director, October 1, 1992.

- Certificate of Appreciation conferred on Emily Peake for her efforts to improve the Stevens Square neighborhood, by the

Board of **Stevens Square Community Organization**, dated December 3, 1992.

- Award to Emily Peake as **Outstanding Indian Senior of 1994** in recognition of her unstinting and unselfish devotion to Seniors. Signed by Darrell Wadena, President of **The Minnesota Chippewa Tribe** and by Gary Frazer, Executive Director, June 3, 1994, at Cass Lake.

- **Minnesota Board on Aging** expresses appreciation to Emily Peake for faithful and dedicated service to all older Minnesotans, particularly all Indian elders. Signed James G. Vargmen, Executive Secretary, and Helen S. Johnston, Chair, 1995.

- **Good Neighbor Award** presented to Emily Peake by WCCO, February 5, 1995.

- Certificate of **Special Congressional Recognition** presented to Emily Peake. Signed Martin Olav Sabo, Fifth District Congressman—Minnesota, April 10, 1995.

- Certificate of **Special Congressional Recognition** presented to Emily Peake in recognition of outstanding and invaluable service to the community. Signed Jim Ramstad, Member of Congress, April 10, 1995.

Bibliography

Allied Commission for Austria, A Handbook, Allied Council, 1949.

Anderson, Gary Clayton, *Little Crow: Spokesman for the Sioux*. St. Paul, MN: Minnesota Historical Society Press, 1986.

Broker, Ignatia, *Night Flying Woman: An Ojibwe Narrative*. St. Paul, MN: Minnesota Historical Society Press, 1983.

Brown, Marshall, Goodwin, Everett, Goodwin, Kathy Roy, Rawley, Jerry, and Wiemer, Georgia, *White Earth: A History*. Cass Lake, MN: The Minnesota Chippewa Tribe.

Brunette, Pauline, "The Minneapolis Urban Indian Community." *Hennepin County History, Winter 1989-90*.

Brunette, Pauline, Buffalohead, Priscilla, DesJarlait, Robert, and Whipple, Naomi, *Ojibwe Family Life in Minnesota: 20th Century Sketches*. Coon Rapids, MN: Anoka-Hennepin School District No.11, 1991.

Cooper, Wyatt, "A Mississippi Memoir," *Town & Country*, May 1978.

Dyer, Frederick H., *A Compendium of the War of the Rebellion*. Des Moines, IA: Dyer Publishing Company, 1908.

Eleff, Bob, "Emily Peake's Roots in Stevens Square Area Are Deep," *The Surveyor* (Minneapolis), December 1990.

Federal Bureau of Investigation (FBI), File No. 121-38349, Emily Peake, 1952.

Folwell, William Watts, *A History of Minnesota, Volume IV*. St. Paul, MN: Minnesota Historical Society, 1930.

Hilger, Sister M. Inez, *A Social Study of White Earth Reservation, 1938*, Reprint Edition. St. Paul, MN: Minnesota Historical Society Press, 1998.

Howell, Terri, "Miracle, The White Buffalo Calf and the Return of Ptesan-Wi," *Pan Gaia*, Summer 2000.

Indians in Minnesota, St. Paul, MN: League of Women Voters of Minnesota, 1974.

LeSueur, Meridel, *Salute to Spring*. New York: International Publishers, 1966.

Littlefield, Daniel F., Jr., and Parins, James W., *A Biobibliography of Native American Writers, 1772-1924*. Metuchen, NJ: The Scarecrow Press, Inc., 1981.

Meyer, Melissa L., *The White Earth Tragedy: Ethnicity and Dispossession at a Minnesota Anishinaabe Reservation*. Lincoln, NE: University of Nebraska Press, 1994.

Minnesota's Indian Citizens, Yesterday and Today, The Governor's Human Rights Commission, State of Minnesota, 1965.

Morris, Lucy Leavenworth Wilder, *Old Rail Fence Corners: Frontier Tales Told by Minnesota Pioneers*, Reprint Edition. St. Paul, MN: Minnesota Historical Society Press, 1976.

Peake, Emily, Grants Program File, 1991, Minnesota Historical Society, St. Paul, MN.

Peake, Emily, "Indian Politics and Power," audio tape in the History Department, Minneapolis Public Library, October 22, 1980.

Pejsa, Jane, "Death in Market Square," *Twin Cities*, April 1985.

Rowland, Dunbar, *Military History of Mississippi, 1803-1898*. Spartanburg South Carolina: The Reprint Company, 1988.

Ross, Hamilton Nelson, *La Pointe: Village Outpost on Madeline Island*. Madison, WI: State Historical Society of Wisconsin, 2000.

Schoemaker, Nancy, "Urban Indians and Ethnic Choices: American Indian Organizations in Minneapolis, 1920-1950," *The Western Historical Quarterly* (Logan, UT), November 1988.

Schultz, Duane, *Over the Earth I Come: The Great Sioux Uprising of 1862*. New York: St. Martin's Press, 1996.

U.S. Army Intelligence, Control No. V-26230, Emily Peake file, 1952.

Vizenor, Gerald Robert, Ed., *Escorts to White Earth: 1868-1968*. Minneapolis, MN: The Four Winds, 1968.

Warren, William W., *History of the Ojibwe People*, Reprint Edition. St. Paul, MN: Minnesota Historical Society Press, 1984.

Westermeyer, Joseph, M.D., Ph.D., and Peake, Emily, "A Ten-Year Follow-Up of Alcoholic Native Americans in Minnesota," *American Journal of Psychiatry*. Washington D.C., February 1983.

Whipple, Henry B., *Lights and Shadows of a Long Episcopate: Being Reminiscences and Recollections of the Right Reverend Henry Benjamin Whipple, Bishop of Minnesota*. New York: The Macmillan Company, 1902.

Wilcox, Alvin H., *A Pioneer History of Becker County*. St. Paul, MN: Pioneer Press Company, 1908.

Periodicals

Indigenous Woman, Spring 1991.

Minneapolis Star, Minneapolis Tribune, Minneapolis Star Tribune, Star Tribune. Minneapolis, MN: various articles, various years.

The Indian Helper, The Indian Craftsman, The Redman, The Carlisle Arrow. Carlisle Indian School, Carlisle, PA, 1891-1914.

The Circle. Minneapolis, MN: various articles, 1989.

The Surveyor, Minneapolis, MN: December 1990.

Selected Internet Sites

American Indian Movement

Buffalo Calf Woman

Carlisle Indian Industrial School History

Enmegahbowh

Handbook of Texas Online

Minneapolis American Indian Center

White Buffalo Woman

White Earth, Minnesota, Ojibwe Reservation

Notes

1. Letter to the Smithsonian dated April 6 and 10, 1910, along with a photocopy of an early interview with Day-Doge. Emily Peake files.

2. Warren, William, *History of the Ojibwe People, Based upon Traditions and Oral Statements*, St. Paul, MN. Minnesota Historical Society, 1885, pp. 44-47.

3. Lucy Leavenworth Wilder Morris, Ed., *Old Rail Fence Corners*, 1976 reprint, St. Paul, MN: Minnesota Historical Society Press, pp. 28, 34.

4. Whipple, Henry, *Lights and Shadows of a Long Episcopate*, New York: MacMillan, 1899, pp. 34–5.

5. Ibid., p. 127.

6. Schultz, Duane, *Over the Earth I Come: The Great Sioux Uprising of 1862.* New York: St. Martin's Press, 1992, p. 42.

7. Broker, Ignatia, *Night Flying Woman, An Ojibwe Narrative*, St. Paul, MN: Minnesota Historical Society Press, 1983, p. 63.

8. Information from *A Pioneer History of Becker County* and family archives.

9. Upham, Warren, *Minnesota Geographical Names, Their Origin and Historical Significance*, Reprint Edition. St. Paul, MN: Minnesota Historical Society, 1969.

10. Published in the Carlisle School alumni newsletter, undated.

11. Folwell, William Watts, *A History of Minnesota, Volume IV,* St. Paul: Minnesota Historical Society, 1930, p. 295.

12. These letters are available from the St. Elizabeth Hospital files at the National Archives in Washington, D.C.

13. Brown, Marshall, etc. *White Earth: A History*, Cass Lake, MN: The Minnesota Chippewa Tribe, p. 37.

14. Folwell, *A History of Minnesota, Volume IV*, cited earlier, chapter entitled "The Tragedy of White Earth"; and Meyer, Melissa L., *The White Earth Tragedy, Ethnicity and Dispossession at a Minnesota Anishinaabe Reservation, 1889-1920*, Lincoln, NE and London, University of Nebraska Press, 1994.

15. From a fragment memoir by Louise Peake, undated.

16. E-mail communication from Frances Green Anderson to the author, June 21, 2002.

17. *The Circle*, February 1989, p. 13.

18. Andy Favorite, White Earth historian, Pine Point, Minnesota.

19. *Minnesota Indian Citizens,Yesterday & Today*, p. 42.

20. *Minneapolis Star,* November 6, 1963.

21. Jeanne Krueger, for 27 years manager of Kenny's Superette on the corner of Clinton and Franklin in the Stevens Square neighborhood.

22. Information gained in an interview with Clyde Bellecourt and from the AIM Web site, "A Brief History of the American Indian Movement," by Laura Waterman Wittstock and Elaine J. Salinas.

23. Author's interview with Thomas Hodne, October 2001.

24. Excerpts from Emily Peake's prepared statement and further conversations with Joe Blade, Staff Writer, *Minneapolis Star*, August 8, 1969.

25. *Minneapolis Star*, January 27, 1970.

26. Warren Wolfe, staff writer, *Minneapolis Tribune*, December 27, 1971, pp. 1B-2B.

27. *Minneapolis Tribune*, April 18, 1973.

28. Upper Midwest American Indian Center minutes, March 13, 1974.

29. Author's interview with Alberta Norris at General Mills, September 7, 2001.

30. *Minneapolis Star and Tribune*, January 27, 1986.

31. *The Surveyor,* December 1990, pp. 7, 14.

32. *Star Tribune*, June 15, 26, 19, and 23, also July 11, 1994.

33. Testimony before the Hennepin County Board of Commissioners, September 19, 1985.

34. Westermeyer, M.D., Ph.D., Joseph and Peake, Emily, "A Ten-Year Follow-Up of Alcoholic Native Americans in Minnesota," *American Journal of Psychiatry* 140:2, February 1983, pp. 189-194.

35. Interview with Joseph Chasing Horse: Howell, Terri, *Pan Gaia*, Summer 2000, pp. 25-28.

36. As remembered by Jacqueline Heine, Emily's niece.

37. Pencil jottings by Jacqueline Heine as she sat with Emily through the night of April 17 to 18, 1995.

Dictionary of Acronyms

AFL	American Federation of Labor
AIM	American Indian Movement
AIOIC	American Indian Opportunity Industrialization Center
BIA	Bureau of Indian Affairs
CCHT	Central Community Housing Trust
CCC	Civilian Conservation Corp
CCC, Inc.	Citizens Community Centers, Inc.
CIO	Congress of International Organizations
FBI	Federal Bureau of Investigation
MAIC	Minneapolis American Indian Center
MUID	Minneapolis Urban Indian Directors
NYA	National Youth Administration
PTA	Parent Teacher Association
SSCO	Stevens Square Community Organization
STAIRS	Service to American Indian Resident Students
UMAIC	Upper Midwest American Indian Center
USCOA	United States Commission for Occupation of Austria
WPA	Work Projects Administration

Index

Note: For Emily Louise Peake and her immediate family—parents Fred & Louise, sister Natalie, and niece Jackie—only first and last pages of citations are recorded here.

Jane Pejsa has written a number of impressive books in the course of her career. A substantial Bush Foundation Award enabled her to research and write *Matriarch of Conspiracy, Ruth von Kleist 1867-1945*, which won both the Minnesota Book Award for Best Biography and the Midwest Independent Publishers' Award for Best Book Overall. It has since appeared in Japanese, German, and most recently in a Polish edition, for which she has received the coveted *Zloty Ekslibris* award in Poland. Her first book, *The Molineux Affair*, was finalist for the Edgar Allan Poe Award, as Best True Crime, presented by the Mystery Writers of America. Both *Gratia Countryman, Her Life, Her Loves, and Her Library* and *Romanoff—Prince of Rogues* were finalists for the Minnesota Book Award, Best Biography. *Romanoff—Prince of Rogues* is currently under a film option.

The Life of Emily Peake marks a return to the midwestern milieu that Pejsa first explored in her biography of the much-loved librarian Gratia Countryman. Emily Peake's long journey from a childhood in Minneapolis, to the post-War environment of occupied Austria, and finally back home to the trials and triumphs of the urban Ojibwe scene, makes for compelling reading. Pejsa brings added resonance to Emily's story by placing it within the broader context of Minnesota and Native American history.